CHRISTIANITY, DEMOCRACY AND COMMUNISM

CHRISTIANITY
DEMOCRACY
AND COMMUNISM

JOHN M. GRAHAM

THE SAINT ANDREW PRESS

EDINBURGH

Printed in Scotland by
Robert Cunningham and Sons Ltd., Alva

Table of Contents

I

The Vision of an Ideal Society

FROM time to time, and especially in times of tyranny or social disorder, men have dreamed of a perfect human society, in which they might dwell in comradely good will, sharing freely the good things of life; a society in which there would be justice for all, even the least; where war would be no more known, power would be united with virtue, and used only to protect the weak, to rebuke the evil-doer, to produce abundance, to nourish the arts, and to promote the innocent enjoyments of a truly civilised existence.

Biblical visions. In the Bible we have such a passage as Isaiah, ch. 2, vv. 1-4, paralleled in Micah, ch. 4, vv. 1-5, and paraphrased in the lovely words of the hymn 'Behold the mountain of the Lord'. We may take these passages together with Isaiah, ch. 11, vv. 1-9. The elements of these visions can be summarised as follows. God will establish His rule through the Messiah reigning as King in Jerusalem over all the nations. Righteousness and peace will flourish under Him. The poor will be sustained, every man enjoying in security his own sufficient property. Nature itself will be transformed: no animal will prey upon another, but all will live together in innocent friendship.

On the face of it, this is pure vision without concrete relation to society as it now exists. There is no suggestion of *how* men might pass from things as they are to this perfection, no account of how the perfect society would function, what institutions it would require. 'The spirit of wisdom, of might and of the fear of the Lord' would bring about and maintain the recreated life of men and beasts. The discontinuity of this

Messianic society with the actual world is emphasised by the references to the animals. A lion eating straw like the ox would have to be anatomically very different from the carnivorous king of the beasts that we know. Yet for all its unreality such a vision can be of great importance. In the context of prophetic teaching as a whole, which was very directly concerned with the moral realities of the political and economic life of the prophets' own times, such a vision makes strong appeal through the imagination to the conscience. It acts as a foil exposing the corruptions, exploitations, enmities and miseries of actual life, and inspires a longing for just and merciful dealing, pointing to the sure foundation of these in the purpose of God.

In the New Testament we have an example of a vision made actual in the book of Acts, ch. 2, where the early Church is described and we are told that 'all that believed were together and had all things common, and sold their possessions and goods, and parted them to all men, as every man had need'. It seems that this early Christian 'communism' was short-lived. The spontaneous uncalculating love of the brethren, generated by their common experience of the grace of God in Christ, expressed itself in this way, it may be, because they expected some immediate ending of the age, and the total transfiguration of life by the coming of the Messianic Kingdom in power. They ceased for the time being to think of provision for the future. This 'communism' of the early Church was certainly not a systematic organisation of economic life as a whole. It concerned not at all the *production* of wealth, nor its *exchange* by way of trade, but simply its *distribution* for use. The whole incident must be regarded as episodic and, in a sense, superficial. It was not an attempt to deal with the permanent problems of the economic life. Indeed it was rather based on the assumption of an escape from the pressure of these problems through the imminence of the new age. It amounted almost to an abandonment of the economic life.

Plato's Republic. Four hundred years before Christ, in Athens, Plato had written a book describing vividly an ideal Republic, in which an important element of communism appears. A very radical form of communism it is, as it affects the life of the highest class in the state. The Republic of Plato's imagination comprises three main classes. The lowest is concerned with economic production, and not much is said about it, except to indicate that it is made up of men and women of inferior quality, and that their place in the social order is to be a strictly subordinate one. They are to be carefully conditioned by an education prescribed by the ruling class and under laws framed by that class. Above the lowest class is one comprising men and women chosen for their energy and courage who would be the auxiliaries of the highest class, undertaking the more active duties of public life, the organisers, administrators and soldiers. Supreme over all are the guardians, chosen for their health, beauty, intelligence and virtue, and carefully trained from birth to fill the highest and most exacting offices—the theorists, law-makers, educators, judges. To ensure their single-minded fidelity to the common wealth these chosen guardians are to be taken from their own parents (who have been eugenically mated to produce them) and brought up with other boys and girls of their own class, neither knowing themselves, nor being known, as the child of this or that father or mother. No less dangerous than the family to the solidarity of the guardian class is the right of private property: so Plato abolishes that too. The guardians live in communal institutions. They cannot amass wealth: their whole life is in the service of the Republic, their whole happiness is to be in the performance of the duties of their station. Plato believes that it will be a great happiness, requiring the exercise of the highest human faculties, and satisfying fully the worthiest human desires.

Here again, no serious attempt is made to relate vision to the realities of life in the Greek state. Incidentally, many searching criticisms are made of the contemporary trends of civic life in Greece. But it is not shown how Athens might become the republic of Plato's dream, except by the suggestion that philosophers should be made kings.[1] In spite of its unreality and extreme doctrines, the *Republic* has continued to occupy an important place in European thought as a fundamental examination of the problems of ethics, politics, education and philosophy, and a stimulus to the imagination.

Thomas More's Utopia. Next only to the *Republic* in fame is the book which has given its name to the whole class of such visions, Sir Thomas More's *Utopia*. This was published in Latin in 1516, and described a perfect society visited by the imaginary narrator, Ralph Hythloday. When the adjective 'utopian' is used nowadays, it carries with it the suggestion of something fascinating but impossibly ideal, and More, himself a man of affairs and Lord Chancellor for Henry VIII, hardly thought of his Utopia as being imitated directly in England. It was written rather as an indirect criticism of the abuses of power in contemporary society and as an expression of the spirit of humanity and reason in the field of law and social order. Not all of the features of Utopia would attract us to apply for citizenship there, but even now its suggestions offer a stimulus to thought. They force us to ask ourselves whether the institutions we accept and the assumptions we make are necessary or desirable. For this the book is well worth reading today.

Experiments in Utopia. Sometimes the attempt has been

1. It is said that Plato himself, at the invitation of its King, was given the chance of applying his theories in a Greek city state of South Italy: but practical politics proved too much for him.

made to give practical realisation to these or similar dreams. The New World of America seemed to offer special opportunities to make a break with the past, and to found in isolation from the evils of old societies, communities which would be built upon the solid foundations of reason and justice, or upon the rock of a pure uncorrupted religion. North American history abounds in attempts of this kind. The Declaration of Independence asserts the rational foundations on which the life of the new state is to be built, the 'self evident' propositions 'that all men are created equal, and that they are endowed by their Creator with certain unalienable rights, and that among these are Life, Liberty and the pursuit of Happiness'. Among many utopian projects in nineteenth-century Britain and America, not a few owed their inspiration to the able and enthusiastic Robert Owen, who worked on the basis of a theory that character is through and through conditioned by institutions and environment.[1] Out of his numerous experiments, themselves mostly failures,[2] arose important developments in trade unionism, education, factory legislation and the co-operative movement. Owen's impatient idealism far outran the possibilities of his time and of ordinary human nature, but he imparted impulses which were given more realistic expression by others. The great weakness of utopianism always is its failure to ask the question 'Where can we go *from here?*' This is illustrated in our own time by an interesting experiment in social vision of the Bruderhof community, which was forced by Hitler's régime in Germany to remove itself to this country. The basic ideas of this Christian community are simple. They believe that modern industrial civilisation has developed a complicated set of human relationships which are beyond the

1. See his *New View of Society*, one of the Everyman Library books.
2. But his New Lanark mills were highly successful and attracted much admiring interest.

control of moral purpose, most of them impersonal and many of them unjust and degrading to human personality. If we are to have a really ethical and religious society, a fresh start must be made. In order that its human relationships may be understood and kept under the control of moral purpose, the society must be simple. This means that it must at least start by being mainly agricultural; such industry as may be allowed must provide opportunity for wholesome creative activity. An open and direct democratic rule by the whole community and the sharing of all but the most immediately personal forms of property are other characteristics. There is something powerfully attractive in the modesty of this approach, and visitors have been greatly impressed by the results. Yet such a community is utopian in two ways. (1) Experience has shown that it can exist only within the protection of the laws of a country like our own: it cannot exist in our actual world by its own strength. (2) Again, it could not be universalised. It can exist only as an island within the greater society of the industrial world which it condemns. A large population like that of Britain could not be supported by the relatively primitive techniques of such agriculture and industry.

Communism as Utopian Vision. In all of the visionary descriptions or experiments in social order to which reference has been made, and in many others that have not been mentioned, communistic elements are to be found in one form or another. Modern Marxist communism is something very different from the communism of Plato, or the Book of Acts, or the Bruderhof, both in theory and practice. Yet we shall make a mistake if we underestimate the element of vision and imaginative aspiration in it, which has given it a certain nobility and attracted to its service many able and devoted men and women. As a symbol of this element of vision we may take the use of the word 'comrade' as a mode

[6]

of address for the highest and lowest. This can become formal and hypocritical. Usually it is applied only within the limits of membership of the working class or even of the Party. Nevertheless it had originally, and keeps yet to some extent, the glow of a genuine ideal. The communist aims at a 'classless' society, where none will have power, and few will have inclination, to exploit their fellows. In that society he believes that the principle will be effective—'from each according to his ability, to each according to his need'. He is convinced that only in that society will men be *truly free*, able to develop their full human powers, released from the pressures of economic necessity and social domination. He ventures even the promise that the State, with its powers of coercion, will become unnecessary and will 'wither away'.

These generous hopes may seem to be 'utopian' in a sense that communism itself condemns and even despises. They may seem to be inconsistent both with human nature and with other elements in communist thought and practice. But they are there, in the classics of communist literature, and as a living element in the communist tradition. They were expressed in the early legislation of the Soviet government, e.g. in the abolition of the death sentence for (non-political) criminal offences and in the setting up of institutions for the reform of the criminal. Another example was the conception, dear to Lenin, of a governmental administration largely in the hands of the people themselves, and in which no one would receive more than an artisan's wages. The presence of such elements in communism has given it, for many who are distressed by the inequities and irrationalities of existing societies, something of the ideal character of a religion.

In spite of this communism repudiates utopianism as a snare and a delusion, a kind of wishful thinking which draws away the attention of men from their present wrongs and frustrations, and keeps them from asking 'Where do we go *from here?'* The distinctiveness of the modern communism of Marx, Lenin and Stalin, with which we are concerned, lies in the claim that it understands the actual social process, and can give effectual guidance and leadership to the working class in its struggle to end exploitation. It is as a realistic down-to-earth fighting force based on thorough-going 'materialism' that it likes to present itself.

How is this paradox to be understood?

with Friedrich Engels, Marx quickly formulated his main theories and gave them powerful expression in the *Communist Manifesto* of 1847. Forced to leave the continent, and finding refuge in England in 1848, where Engels was already well established (oddly enough as a successful business man), he thenceforward made his whole life's work the understanding of the process of social development with a view to guiding the action of the working class. London was his headquarters. In 1864 he formed and directed for the eight years of its active existence the International Working Men's Association (the First International). In 1867 he published the first part of *Capital* (*Das Kapital*), which was to become the authoritative theoretical basis of communism. He lived a life of meagre comfort, strenuous study, and active controversy, till his death and burial at Highgate in 1883.

The materialist, dialectical and historical elements in Marx's theories were all derived from predecessors. What was new (and what gave a new meaning also to these ideas derived from others), was the emphasis put upon the *economic* factor in social development, and the linking up of theory to the organisation of working class power.

The Economic Interpretation of History. Getting a livelihood is the first and remains the most constant interest of men. The means they adopt to get a livelihood and the relations with other men that are developed in the process, decide the basic patterns of human life in society. This is what gives the foundation structure to society. On top of this, a super-structure may be built, in which morals, religion, law, education, science, philosophy, art, all have their places. But all these interests exist within conditions that are imposed by the state of development of the economic life. The relations of production determine all other relations within society.

Ever since the breakdown of a supposed prehistoric primitive communism, the economic process has resulted in a society divided into economic classes. Freeman and slave, patrician and plebeian, lord and serf, gildmaster and journeyman, landlord and tenant, capitalist and wage-earning worker; such at various epochs are types of the class divisions into which society has been split. All these class relationships involve antagonism between the classes concerned in them. History is a succession of class struggles. Any period of relative stability is one in which one class, enjoying a favourable position, has been able to dominate and to exploit the other classes.

This domination is exercised in various ways. Economic advantage is reinforced by state power. Laws are framed and administered in such ways as to protect the privileges of the exploiting class, while keeping the minimum of order and contentment which may be necessary to make society function. The conflict of interest between the classes remains as a factor of instability, a contradiction within society, the cohesion of which must, therefore, be maintained by force. The police and army are of the essence of the class State.

Not only so; the ruling class must also carry its exploitation into the field of ideas, building up and maintaining a system of beliefs and precepts which supports and justifies the class structure on which their domination depends. The intelligentsia, the priesthood, the official class (bureaucracy) are brought into service as dependants sharing some of the privileges of the ruling class.

The relations thus described are *dialectical* in character. The stability of society contains a tension, the unity conceals an opposition, and that tension and opposition develop sooner or later into a disruption and conflict out of which arises in due course a new synthesis. Concretely, changes in the basic economic processes enable some element in the exploited classes to strengthen its position to the point at which it can carry through a revolutionary struggle and, with the aid of other exploited elements, break the power of the ruling class, and establish itself in the dominant position. A change in economic relationships thus produces consequent changes in political constitution, in law and morals, in religious ideas, in artistic forms and in the direction given to science. Thus the increased importance of commerce, banking and manufactures as compared with agriculture led to the strengthening of the middle class (third estate, bourgeoisie), who rose into power in a series of revolutions, ostensibly religious (Reformation), cultural (Enlightenment) and political (French Revolution), but reflecting in every case an underlying shift of economic power.

The Proletarian Revolution. There is in Marx's thought an optimistic element which certainly does not arise from his basic materialism, but reflects the experience of the times in which he lived and wrote. It was a period of venture and expansion for Europe and especially for Britain. Karl Marx discerned in the dialectical movement of history (here following Hegel), a progress towards higher forms of social life. Capitalism was more productive than agrarian feudalism, and so a stage towards the setting free of men from the necessities that ruled their lives. But capitalism has brought society to a stage of development which is of very special importance to history as a whole, because it is the stage in which the lowest class of all, the wage-earning working class, is developing inevitably, by the very nature of capitalism, a self-consciousness and an organisation in defence of its interests, which will enable it to overthrow the capitalist class, and to take its place of dominance.

How this would come about he envisaged in the following manner. Capitalist development involves (he believed) the concentration of capital in fewer and fewer hands. The smaller capitalist is squeezed out and depressed to the ranks of the proletariat. The struggle between proletariat and capitalists becomes sharper, and the issue between them becomes clearer. It becomes an open conflict for the possession of the sources of economic power and it can end only when the proletariat 'expropriates the expropriators' and takes over the means of production *as a common property*. In order to do so effectively the institutions by which the capitalists maintain themselves in power would have to be destroyed, and replaced by institutions appropriate to a classless society. This process of revolutionary change would be resisted and whatever force was necessary to overcome that resistance would have to be used. The period of transition would require the exercise of dictatorial powers by the proletariat before the new society had been securely established.

It was in connection with the preparation of the working class for the carrying out of this operation, and for the leadership of that class through the period of revolution that Marx began to develop the ideas which later crystallised in the formation of the Communist Party. He himself did not found the Communist Party, but he wrote and spoke a great deal about the strategy and tactics of contemporary revolutionary and semi-revolutionary groups in this and in other countries. He strove to get them to learn from their failures and to be guided in future by his analysis of the situation of the working class. He tried above all to persuade them that their inevitable position in capitalism involves them in irreconcilable war with the ruling class. They must accept these conditions and conduct their struggle without illusions, the illusions that arise from patriotism, from religion, from morality. Across the frontiers of the nation-states the working class is one in its interests and should be united in its organisation and its strategy.

These ideas played a dominant part in the creation of the Social Democratic Parties of various countries, notably in Germany in the late nineteenth and early twentieth centuries.

In due time they were taken up by certain of the revolutionary forces which had been created in Russia by the tyranny of the Czars, and through them made their momentous impact on the West in our own generation.

Before leaving Marx it should be said that beyond this naked struggle of rival powers in the proletarian revolution, he saw wonderful new possibilities opening out before men. He believed it would be possible in a co-operative classless society enormously to increase the production of wealth to the point at which there would be made actual the state of things indicated in the formula 'from each according to his ability, to each according to his need'. The compulsive power of the state would become superfluous. Men would be set free from the constraints of hunger and fear; the brutish peasant would be liberated from his bondage to the soil and associated with the enlightenment and culture of the cities. So different would life become that all that had gone before would seem to belong to an age before history. The true history of man, free at last to be himself and cultivate his highest powers, would begin. At this point we return to the undoubted element of utopian vision in communism even of the Marxist sort.

III

An Expectation Falsified by Events

MORE than 100 years have passed since Marx first published the *Communist Manifesto*, and more than 80 since he worked out his ideas more fully in *Capital*. These years have brought great transformations in the economic and political systems of the countries he chiefly studied. How do these changes correspond with his anticipations?

According to Marxist teaching, history moves through a *dialectical* process of change. From this point of view, capitalism itself is a stage, and it would seem, a necessary stage, on the way to communism. Capitalist development of the productive forces, capitalist organisation of large economic units, capitalist regimentation of wage-earning workers, represent an advance on previous economic systems, yielding a greater output of wealth. At the same time, capitalist society inevitably increases the contradictions inherent in its own structure, to the point of producing breakdown, leading to revolution. For example, in Marx's view, the accumulation of capital is achieved by denying to the workers their due share in the product of their work. But this means that increasingly the accumulated capital cannot be profitably employed, because the impoverished workers cannot buy the goods they produce. So the conflict of interest between capitalists and workers is bound to become more obvious and more acute. The contradiction between the dependence of capitalists on the workers and their denial of the interests of the workers is for Marx an ineradicable feature of capitalism. It can be resolved only by the revolutionary transformation of capitalism into communism, the

[18]

essence of which is the taking over of the ownership of all capital, all the means of production, distribution and exchange, as a common or social property of the workers themselves.

From all this it follows, and Marx himself drew this conclusion, that it would be in the most advanced capitalist countries that the revolution leading to communism would take place.

On the face of it, history has failed to justify these anticipations. The most advanced capitalist countries are just those that have been least seriously threatened with the prospect of revolution, while the revolutions that have taken place under the banner of Marx have occurred in countries meagrely developed as capitalist economies.

How is this to be explained?

Britain's Development Since Marx's Time. Let us look first at Britain. When Marx was forming his ideas, there was much in this country to support his interpretation. The period from 1832 to 1854 has been described by J. L. and Barbara Hammond as the 'Bleak Age'. The capital which brought to Britain the great wealth and power of the later Victorian period was being accumulated then under conditions very hard and miserable for many thousands of the working people—long hours of toil in unwholesome workplaces, squalid housing densely overcrowded, and cruel neglect of those who, in fiercely competitive conditions, lost their work or their health. Harsh practice was supported by harsh theory. It was believed that wages were determined by an 'iron law', and that the only way to ensure economic progress was to leave these economic laws to operate without legislative interference (e.g. compulsory limitations of hours), or even philanthropic intervention. Labour often was regarded as a marketable commodity, to be bought as cheaply as possible and exploited fully in production. To the economist labour was a 'factor of production', along with land and capital. The 'surplus value' theory of Marx, the theory that the capitalist returned to the labourers in wages only enough to secure a continued supply of labour, and appropriated to himself all the value of the product of industry beyond this, might well have seemed at that time very nearly to be a description of the facts.

But prominent as were these features of capitalist industrial progress in Britain, there were present also other social forces of great importance.

(1) There were men who protested vehemently against the harsh theories of capitalism, the theories of unfettered individualistic competition and the free play of supply and demand which are summed up in the phrase 'laissez-faire'. Men like Thomas Carlyle, and later John Ruskin and William Morris, whose writings had wide influence, expressed their scorn for the 'dismal science' of political economy with its inhuman concern for *things*, and its unconcern for *men*. They, and many others, insisted that labour means a labourer (and his family), a *man* with the feelings, the needs and the rights of a man. The moral basis of all social life was powerfully expounded in speech and writing and illustrated in practice by men like Thomas Arnold, the great headmaster of Rugby, F. D. Maurice, theologian, and Charles Kingsley, preacher and novelist.

(2) In a more directly practical way, Chadwick, Shaftesbury, Florence Nightingale and many others (themselves belonging to the privileged classes) forced upon the attention of Parliament the suffering and degradation of the poor, and secured substantial reforms.

(3) The workers themselves developed in their trade unions an organisation which greatly strengthened their bargaining power in negotiation with their employers.

(4) The system of representative government was adapted by stages from 1832 onwards to include as electors, and later

as members of Parliament, those who could give expression in law and administration to the needs and claims of the populations of the new industrial areas. First as the Radical wing of the Liberal Party, and, from 1900 onwards, in an independent Labour Party, the working people were able to exert an increasing pressure on government to secure their own interests and progress.

(5) The capitalist industrial and commercial system under these influences proved itself capable of great expansion, developing with the help of science new resources of wealth which have allowed of substantial improvements in the standard of living of the workers.

So in Britain, in America, in the British Dominions and in Western Europe, social development has taken a course very different from the anticipations of Karl Marx, and his theories have not until quite recently made much impression in this country. Indeed they have made their impact mainly through the fact that they became the creed of the successful revolutionaries of Russia.

The Causes of the Russian Revolution. Up to 1917, the Russian Empire, comprising vast territories inhabited by peoples of many languages and races, at very different stages of material and cultural achievement, was ruled by an autocratic monarch assisted by an aristocracy of great landowners and a small middle class bureaucracy, in close alliance with a conservative church. Russia had lived for centuries on the edge of European civilisation, half isolated, half Asiatic. She had experienced neither the Renaissance nor the Reformation. The influence of the West had reached her in the early eighteenth century through the Czar, Peter the Great, whose chief interest was in technical progress, and whose political tyranny was as absolute as that of any of his predecessors. In the later eighteenth and in the nineteenth century, the intellectuals of Russia were greatly influenced by the ideas of

Voltaire, Darwin, Herbert Spencer—that is by ideas which tended towards materialistic and atheist interpretations of human life.[1] It was only late in the nineteenth century that Russia began to develop industrially, with the aid of French, German and British capital. Right up to the Revolution more than 80 per cent of her people were peasants, many of them not far removed from serfdom, which was not legally abolished till 1861.

A very remarkable feature of the nineteenth and early twentieth centuries in Russia was the number of people, members of what they themselves called the 'intelligentsia', who were in more or less active rebellion against the social institutions and the dominant religious and moral traditions of their own country. The inflexible conservatism of these institutions was supported by the irresponsible power of the autocracy. A situation developed in which numbers of able men and women could find no satisfactory expression for themselves in the culture, administration or economic life of their society. Repressed by a heavy censorship, spied upon by a secret police organisation, they could neither in speech, writing nor action move outside the limits prescribed by government. They were driven to extreme views, and, in many cases, to subversive and violent action. Some associated themselves with the oppressed peasants, either, like Tolstoy, seeing in the simplicity of the country man's life something wholesome to be imitated, or offering themselves as leaders in a general revolt against the oppressive tyranny of the Czars, from which, in their different ways, peasants and intellectuals both suffered.

Among these intellectuals we are here specially concerned with one man, Vladimir Ilyich Ulanov, born in 1870 in the middle Volga region. His people were of a middle class

1. For an account of the intellectual *Origins of Russian Communism* see the book of this title by Nicolas Berdiaev.

status. While he was a senior pupil at school, his brother Alexander was executed for his part in a conspiracy of Moscow students against the Czar. In 1905, the year of the defeat of the Czar's forces by the Japanese, discontent was rife, and expressed itself in various places in demonstrations and demands for limited reforms. These demands were at first conceded in part, and then the authority of the Czar was reasserted in a series of arbitrary and cruel repressive measures. During the period between 1905 and 1914, there was throughout Europe a development of industry and trade in which the leading parts were taken by Britain, Germany and France, in increasing rivalry with one another for the markets of the world and for the control of colonial territories. To a limited extent Russia shared in this development and France sought to strengthen itself vis-à-vis Germany by an alliance with the Russian autocracy, which was supported by loans, while at the same time British, German and American capital sought profitable outlets for investment in the petroleum, gold mining, textile, coal and iron and other industries of Russia.

Under these conditions an industrial proletariat was developing, which offered a field for the activities of the revolutionary forces, but always under the hampering conditions of the inflexible repressive system of Czarist rule. Much of the revolutionary agitation had to be conducted from places of exile abroad. In this way Ulanov, now known as Lenin, took a leading part. In Russia itself, agitation, organisation of strikes and demonstrations, printing and distribution of papers and pamphlets, all alike illegal, were conducted by men whose activity was frequently interrupted by long terms of imprisonment or exile in remote districts of Siberia. Such a revolutionary, working under the leadership of Lenin, was Joseph Djugashvili, a Georgian, later to be known as Stalin. The conditions of their life bred in these men habits of secrecy, ruthlessness and suspicion which remained with them in their later years of power.

The Bolsheviks. It was during this period that Lenin emerged as the intellectual leader and master strategist of those revolutionary elements which were linked most closely to the industrial workers of Russia. They formed the Social Democratic Party based on the theories of Karl Marx. Within this party a series of struggles took place between two main groups, the Bolsheviks ('majority') and the Mensheviks ('minority'). The difference between these groups centred on the question of the organisation of the party itself. Broadly speaking, the Menshevik conception was not unlike the western idea of a democratic political party. They thought its leadership and policy should be decided by the rank and file membership through free recruitment, free discussion and free voting. Lenin, on the other hand, developed quite a different view of the role and structure of the party of Socialist revolution. His thought of it was *controlled by the concept of class war*, which was of course central to Marxist theory. A party capable of leading the proletariat in its war against the ruling class must have the highly disciplined organisation and something of the temper of an army. The implications of this comparison are clear: the direction of an army is in the hands of a general staff, its officers and N.C.O.s must be reliable, and no risks can be taken even with the rank and file. Out of this conception there developed the Bolshevik (later, the Communist) Party, with a highly centralised organisation, a harsh and powerful discipline, secret plans, and other features more characteristic of military than political organisation.

The Course of the Revolution in Russia. In 1914 Russia was involved in war with Germany and the Austrian Empire, France and Britain being her allies in the West. By the end of 1916 military defeat, immense loss and suffering, increasing disorganisation both military and economic, provoked wide-spread discontent, which expressed itself in political revolution in February 1917. The overthrow of the Czar was led by liberal aristocratic and middle class elements and their aim was to replace autocratic government by parliamentary democracy, while continuing the war. Their task under prevailing conditions was perhaps impossible. The Russian people had almost no experience of representative self-government and the war was increasingly unpopular. The German Government and Army exploited the situation by increasing its pressure on the Eastern Front, and by arranging for the return from his Swiss exile of Lenin, hoping for his intervention to result in the withdrawal of Russia from the War.

Alongside the Parliamentary institutions which were struggling into precarious life, there grew rapidly and spontaneously in factories, villages and towns, and even among the military formations, what were called soviets (councils), loose organisations formed to voice complaints and make demands of all sorts against landlords, government and superior officers. Under Lenin's guidance the Bolsheviks, a relatively small but resolute and disciplined party, set to work to achieve the leadership of the soviets, seeing in them a potentially overwhelming social force. The strategy of the Bolsheviks was to give coherence and organisation to the soviets, to unify their demands through 'slogans', or simple headline statements of their aims, and to occupy key positions on their executive committees. They helped to crystallise the aspirations of the soviets round the demands for peace, bread, and the land for the peasants. Eventually it was in the name of the soviets that the Provisional Government of the February Revolution was dispossessed of its authority in the great cities of Russia in October 1917 and a new Revolutionary Government set up.

The soviets were not Bolshevik, nor even Marxist. In the countryside the party of 'Social Revolutionaries' was predominant in influence, and Menshevik and other groups played an important part everywhere, in many places predominating in numbers among those committed to a distinct party affiliation. But the Bolsheviks now reaped the harvest of Lenin's training. In the confusions of the time, they were the best disciplined, the most resolutely led, the most single minded political organisation. Their greatest asset was Lenin himself, and next to him in power of personality was Trotsky, who grew rapidly in influence when he was given the task of organising and directing the new Red Army in the defence of the revolutionary régime.

The detailed history of the Revolution and of the years of its consolidation and development is worthy of study. Here certain broad features only require mention.

1. It was accomplished only in the face of bitter armed opposition, which was supported by the Western Allies, who not only sent arms to the counter-revolutionary armies, but themselves intervened with military forces, and after their failure and withdrawal refused for some years to recognise the new Soviet government.

2. The various revolutionary parties agreed broadly on a 'socialist' programme involving some form of public state ownership of factories, banks and transport undertakings, but organisation was necessarily for a long time incomplete, provisional and far from uniform. All sorts of revolutionary ideas concerning marriage, crime, religion, government, industry, agriculture, were competing for expression in a chaotic situation. One supremely important question had never been thought out by the Bolsheviks clearly, viz. the role of the peasants in a socialist state. As Marxists their interest was primarily in the industrial worker—the proletariat of capitalist society. Yet Russia was 80 per cent a

peasant society and the success of the revolution was dependent on peasant support. Meantime the land was left in the hands of the peasants in a mixed ownership partly individual and family property, partly under the control of the village community or *mir*. The question of agriculture and the peasant under Communism was later to be among the most stubborn problems.

3. For some years hopes were high that the Revolution would spread to other countries, and especially to Germany. When these hopes continued to be disappointed, acute disagreement developed regarding the policy to be adopted by the International Communist Party, Comintern, which had been founded in 1919 to encourage the revolution in all countries.

4. The dominance of the Bolshevik over other revolutionary parties was gradually secured by methods which included terror and the use of an increasingly powerful secret police. But so long as Lenin lived, disagreements and rivalries within the Bolshevik party itself remained more or less latent. His authority was very great, great enough even to allow him to make a strategic retreat in the economic organisation of the Soviet Union in 1923, which involved the revival of elements of capitalism to assist the recovery of Russia from the desperate condition of poverty into which war, revolution and civil war had brought her people. This was described as the New Economic Policy (N.E.P.).

When Lenin died after a long illness in 1924, he was treated as a kind of Bolshevik saint. His embalmed body was laid in a mausoleum in Moscow's Red Square and became an object of veneration. His teaching was regarded as above question and his writings (with those of Marx) have ever since been a court of final appeal in every controversy.

IV

The Development of Communist Society under Joseph Stalin (1)

As its authority was slowly and painfully established, and the Bolshevik or Communist Party government became more able to decide on its future policy, it was faced with a situation for which Marxist theory gave very incomplete guidance. It had been part of that theory that the proletarian revolution would arise out of a situation created by capitalism. That is to say, it would take place in a well-developed capitalist economy, and the proletariat would inherit its advanced technology, its great industrial installations, its transport, its commercial institutions, not undamaged, but capable of quick repair. In the classless society, without the conflicts arising from the opposed interests of capitalists and workers, these resources would be used with a new energy and singlemindedness and would become rapidly more productive, yielding for the consumers of their products a constantly improving standard of life.

What had happened was quite different. The Russian economy was far more agricultural than industrial, its social system more feudal than capitalist, its industrial and technological resources slender. After the impoverishment and confusions of years of war and civil conflict, it was hardly even a going concern.

How were the new rulers, the leaders of the Communist Party, to envisage their task?

1. They might reckon that the first necessity was to restore as soon as possible the material standards of life of the people.

2. They might try to demonstrate in new institutions the

freedom of which many of the revolutionaries had dreamed; factories controlled by their own workers; marriages contracted and dissolved according to the free choice of the men and women directly concerned; popular government at every level with no bureaucracy and no professional army—a citizen administration, a citizen army; prisons that would reform rather than punish the criminal; and so on.

3. They might devote themselves to promoting the revolution in other countries, by supporting foreign communist parties and diplomatic intervention.

4. They might give first place to building up the economic and military strength of the Soviet Union through large scale development of the heavy industries.

In a sense, all of these things had to be done or attempted, but which should be regarded as most important? Among the leaders of the Communists different views were held. Also, there were keen personal rivalries amongst them. Which policies, and which leaders, were to prevail?

We have seen that Lenin had shaped his Party in accordance with the principle of 'democratic centralism'. The central executive organs of the Party were elected by the Party membership, and had to submit their policy to the Party for approval. *But*, the central executive was given power not only to carry out the approved policy, but to give the necessary orders to the members in doing so, and to supervise and discipline the members in respect both of their actions and their opinions. This allowed the men at the centre a power which could be used to suppress by expulsion any members of the party holding minority views or otherwise challenging their leadership. Lenin could be very ruthless in dealing with 'reactionary elements' and 'class enemies' outside the party, or with doubtful or difficult persons or groups within it. To some extent, these drastic powers had been necessitated by the practice common in

Czarist days of planting 'agents provocateurs' within the Revolutionary parties to find out what they were plotting and to provoke them to actions that would expose them and lead to the punishment of their leaders and the destruction of their organisation. Nevertheless, Lenin tolerated some diversity of views within the party. His authority as a leader enabled him to do this. But with Lenin gone, a struggle for leadership ensued, in which Trotsky and Stalin were the main figures, with others deeply involved.

It is important to recognise the nature of this struggle. The Communist Party, we have seen, had something of the character of an army, waging a war against its class enemies. This implied for its members that they must *obey*, without question, the orders of their leaders—'theirs not to reason why'. A soldier is not allowed to resign or desert because he disagrees with the plan of campaign or the battle orders. He must accept the plan and the place assigned to him in it. If he fails in obedience or loyalty, he will be severely punished, perhaps shot. The army must present a solid front to the foe. So the militant Communist Party, the trained cadres of the proletariat, must have a 'monolithic' unity; there must be no crack or joint or soft spot where a wedge can be driven in to split and break it up.

A political party with us is something quite different from this. Its discipline is easy, and never summarily exercised. Any serious difference of views is dealt with by discussion leading to a compromise, which will unite the maximum number of members. Remaining minorities may resign, but often they retain their membership while for the time being they go into the background, emerging perhaps later to resume their activity when changing circumstances have brought them nearer to the majority view on the issue of the day.

We find this tolerance possible because our political parties are not based on dogmas, but on general ideas and common sympathies and interests. It is not thought among us that there is only one 'correct' answer to a political problem. We assume rather that there may be various reasonably good ways of achieving an end, and that only experience can show whether any of them is as good as it looks to its advocates. In Marxism the belief that political action can and must be guided by 'correct' and 'scientific' theory, and can be deduced in a given situation from Marxist first principles, leads to the conclusion that a minority view is not only different, but must be 'incorrect' and therefore dangerous and requiring suppression.

In this context we can understand that it is a matter of supreme importance to a Communist to be one of the majority in his Party, or, rather, more precisely, to be in agreement with the doctrines and policies decided upon by the most powerful central organ of the Party. I say 'the most powerful central organ' because that body can always ensure (by its disciplinary control of the membership lower down) majority support at any general congress of the Party. The struggle within the Communist Party for the control of its central organs has, therefore, been, since the death of Lenin, intense: indeed, it has been of murderous intensity. In its course through many tortuous phases, all of the leaders of any eminence in the Revolution, with the exception of Lenin and Stalin (who was not then at all pre-eminent) have suffered ignominy, expulsion, imprisonment, exile, torture or death, and their fate has been shared by hundreds, thousands, even tens and hundreds of thousands, of their followers or associates in the Party.

Some Phases of the Internecine Struggle of the Communist Party

(1) *Stalin v. Trotsky.* Ostensibly, the struggle always concerned the 'correct' policy or 'party line'. In reality, it often

was more concerned with personal rivalry for leadership. This is clearly shown by the shifts of policy of particular leaders, designed to secure the support of others.

The first, and most bitter and far reaching conflict, between Trotsky and Stalin, developed round the question—How is the Russian revolution related to the revolution in other countries? Theoretically the revolution should not have occurred in Russia at all—a country of peasants—but in Britain, in Germany, or some such advanced 'capitalist' country. So long as the Soviet Union was surrounded by such natural enemies as the powerful capitalist countries its overthrow was possible, or even probable. Certainly, if even one of the great capitalist states had come under proletarian dictatorship led by its Communist Party, it would have immensely strengthened the revolution in Russia. Economic development could have gone on much more rapidly, and the military security of the Soviet government would have been enhanced. (Even as things turned out, the Soviet Union had to get the help of German, British, American and other technical experts in carrying through its major industrial projects.) Trotsky, therefore, insisted that a prime object of communist strategy must be the extension of the revolution. Another way of putting the same view is that international communism (the Comintern, or federation of communist parties) must be dominant over the Communist Party of the Soviet Union, and there were many implications of great importance for Russia in this view, in both foreign and domestic policy.

Stalin, who had been only once or twice outside the limits of Soviet territory on special revolutionary missions, conceived the possibility of building up the new communist society in the Soviet Union in relative isolation from the rest of the world: 'socialism in one country alone'. By reducing contact with the outer world, maintaining an iron control of the people, by concentrating on development of the heavy industries first, the Soviet Union with its vast territories and resources could complete its revolution alone. Some help would be needed from capitalist countries, but that could be got by bargaining. As for the Comintern (although this was never made explicit) the logic of Stalin's policy was that it should become an instrument of the Soviet Communist Party, and its activities directed to the strengthening of the Soviet Union.[1]

In Russia, Stalin's theory would seem more realistic and congenial. But more important than the persuasiveness of his theory was the fact that Stalin occupied the key position in the central executive organs of the Party, General Secretary, member of the Politburo and secretary of the special committee charged with the duty of party organisation and discipline. Stalin had to fight hard against various combinations among the Bolshevik leaders, against strong forces of discontent in Russia and against notable leaders of international communism. In overcoming them he employed methods of intrigue, defamation and violence which had an important effect on the Communist Party and on the Russian people.

1. It was argued that the best way to ensure the triumph of the Revolution in other countries was *first of all* to defend and build up the Communist régime in Russia. This was accepted by many communists in Britain, Germany and other countries, and they became completely subservient to the decisions of the Politburo of the Soviet Communist Party. Those who tried to maintain an independent judgment in regard to the role of their own national communist parties were sometimes very brutally handled by the Soviet Secret Police. See Ruth Fischer's book on German communism. Trotsky himself was eventually assassinated *in Mexico* by an agent of the Soviet Secret Police. The most striking illustration of the subservience of the British Communist Party was given at the beginning of the war in 1939. Pollitt completely reversed his position within a month to bring himself in line with the instructions of the Moscow H.Q. of Communism.

(2) *The Struggle with the Peasants.* It has already been observed that Marx, and those who accepted his 'scientific' analysis of society, had never succeeded in finding a satisfactory place for the peasant in the revolution, nor in the classless society. On the one hand, they always spoke as if the proletariat was the last and lowest exploited class, and yet almost in the same breath spoke of the peasantry as an inferior kind of proletariat, backward, ignorant and incapable of revolutionary initiative. Marx had failed to anticipate that the peasantry could itself be a revolutionary class, and that its revolutionary programme might be very different from that of the urban proletariat. In fact, the revolution in Russia was at least partly a vast spontaneous uprising of the peasants until its leadership was adroitly and resolutely seized by Lenin's well disciplined party. Lenin secured the support of the peasants by agreeing that they should take possession of the land for themselves *as a private property.* This was from the point of view of communism a dangerous concession. It meant that, in one vast sector of the economy, the Revolution was based on private property in the means of production, a contradiction of the socialist principle, and a base from which, conceivably, 'capitalism' might launch a reactionary attack on communist leadership. The concession was made, because it was believed that the Bolsheviks, with control of the state power (law, army, police, etc.) and of the 'commanding heights' of the economic system (great industries, issue of money, etc.), would be able in due course to *reverse* the situation in the countryside. This possibility was based on the belief (not borne out by much of the evidence) that the most productive agriculture is large scale mechanised farming.[1] It was anticipated that, by creating huge farms, and

1. The technological basis for large-scale mechanised farming hardly existed in Russia at this period (1928-33). Not only was the supply of agricultural machinery insufficient, but the peasants were unaccus-

running them on industrial lines, like factories, the peasants could be attracted into them by good wages, and that in the process they would be assimilated to the proletariat of the towns. Not only so, but the farms would become more dependent on the towns which would supply, service, and distribute the tractors and combine-harvesters, etc., and provide them with oil fuel.

Opposition might arise from the richer peasants (Kulaks) who had profited most from the private exploitation of the land, but this could be broken by the superior numbers of the poorer peasants who would flock into the collective farms.

Such was the theory. During the period of civil war, to feed the towns and the Red Army, forcible requisitioning of crops was frequent, and the peasants were alienated and many became hostile to the Bolshevik régime. After the civil war, shortages of food and clothing were on a catastrophic scale; the whole standard of life of the people, in town and country, had fallen to a level of misery. To feed the people, and to pay, by the sale of grain abroad, for the machines that would begin the building up of Soviet industry, a vast increase in farm production both of foodstuffs and industrial raw materials (cotton, wool, etc.) was urgent. Lenin had met this situation by his New Economic Policy, giving an opportunity of private profit to the farmer, which the more intelligent and energetic were not slow to take. But the more successful this policy proved, the more it consolidated the interest of the countryside in private property and contradicted the Communist basis of the Revolution.

Stalin in launching the first Five Year Plan in 1928 decided to include in it a big programme of collectivisation of the farms. It was undoubtedly his assumption that technically

tomed to its use. Even the number of draught animals on the farms was far below requirements.

this was the most productive method in agriculture, but that, of course, depended on the goodwill of the peasants. This proved to be lacking. The Soviet authorities found themselves faced by a stubborn opposition to their plans. Rather than yield up their family ownership of the farms, and sell their crops and cattle at prices fixed to suit the government's plans, many of the peasants destroyed their beasts and reduced their sowings.

The bitterness of the struggle was not realised at the time outside the Soviet Union, nor even everywhere within it. In Russia nothing is published without Party approval and the situation was disguised by the official pretence that only the rich peasants were involved in opposition and they were, of course, described as class enemies, wreckers, traitors and saboteurs of the programme of socialist construction. In fact, opposition in some of the richest agricultural regions seems to have been widespread, and was overcome only by the most extreme measures. In the process extensive famines desolated these regions, whole communities were 'liquidated' by imprisonment, exile or death, and the suffering affected millions of people. Agricultural production fell away and the drive for collectivisation had for a while to be relaxed. Eventually, by incessant propaganda, some concessions, and relentless pressure of the state power, a considerable degree of collectivisation has been achieved and the productivity of agriculture has slowly risen to more adequate levels, but not even now has the level of nutrition reached Western standards.

The struggle with the peasants caused stresses within the Communist Party, but less than might be imagined, because the peasants had never been numerous in the Party membership, and proportionately even less in its leading positions. Marxism from the beginning has tended to think of the peasants, not as equal partners with the proletariat, still less as a distinct economic class with its own interests different from those of the proletariat, but rather as subordinate allies, somehow to be fitted into plans conceived in proletarian terms.

The peasant problem continues to plague the communist régimes of all the East European countries, which, like Russia, remain, to this day, predominantly peasant in composition.

(3) *The Struggle with the Trade Unions.* Another illustration of the divided counsels of the Communist Party of the Soviet Union is to be found in the trade unions. In the Russia of the Czars, trade unions were never, as they have long been in Britain, powerful organisations with established legal rights. But they developed quickly to play a part in the Revolutionary reorganisation of Soviet industry. From the trade union standpoint, the Revolution meant workers' control of industry in one form or another. The first attempts at direct management of factories by their workers proved impracticable, but even after their failure trade unionists expected a degree of independence for themselves and a big say in industrial policy.

There developed, therefore, a struggle between those in the Communist Party whose power rested on their leadership of the trade unions (such as Tomsky) and those whose power depended on control of the Party organisation itself, the chief being Stalin. Again Stalin, by superior skill in political tactics, and his ability to use all the resources of press, police and Party, overwhelmed his opponents. Tomsky acknowledged defeat in suicide.

V

The Development of Communist Society under Joseph Stalin (2)

IT is often said that it is difficult or even impossible to find out what has actually developed in the Soviet Union out of the communist revolution. This difficulty is sometimes attributed to the hostility of 'capitalist' newspapers and publishing firms, which are supposed to be united in a conspiracy of silence regarding the unexampled progress of the only socialist society in the world. In fact there is no censorship, official or unofficial, on the publication of such information in a country like ours. A great deal has been written, from journalistic reports to massive technical studies, much of it with a highly favourable bias, much of it by British communists, some indeed directly published by the Soviet Embassy. Anyone can buy his *Daily Worker*, or subscribe to the *Labour Monthly*. There is no very formidable barrier here to anyone who can write well telling all he knows about life in the Soviet Union.

The real difficulty is in finding out in the U.S.S.R. itself freely and fully what is happening there. All the means of information there are strictly controlled by government and Party. News items which are at once published in the free press of the Western World may be held up for days, or never published at all, at the direction of the government. Movement into and out of the U.S.S.R. is controlled with the utmost vigilance and strictness. Movement within Russia by any foreigner is restricted, supervised or indirectly limited in extreme degree.[1] The policy of the Soviet authori-

---

1. Soviet citizens are generally wary and evasive in their contacts with all foreigners.

ties has been to seal off their own people from all but the most necessary contacts with the outside world. Only very recently has this been somewhat relaxed.

There are, therefore, many things in the Soviet Union about which exact and up-to-date information is not available to us. But it is easy to exaggerate the extent of our ignorance. The mystery is not complete and broad conclusions can be reached, on the basis of verified facts, on most important matters.

The two matters on which Soviet communism makes the most challenging claims are (1) economic progress and (2) social justice.

(1) *Economic Progress.* One part of the indictment of capitalist society (made not only by Communists) concerns the high degree of anarchy evident in the economic life of the most advanced capitalist countries. It is contended by many (and denied by others) that this is inherent in capitalism and incurable under that system. Two elements in the indictment can be distinguished: (i) Considered merely as a productive system, the economic organisation of capitalism has from time to time suffered partial (and for many people disastrous) breakdown. After years of activity and expansion have come years of slump. Factories have been forced to close, banks have failed, millions of men have been thrown out of employment, ground has been left uncultivated. (ii) Considered as a means of supplying human needs, the indictment of capitalism is that even at the height of its activity, in a period of boom, a capitalist economy leaves many of the most fundamental human needs in neglect, while its processes are directed to the pursuit of profit for the investor, towards the multiplication of luxuries. In times of depression productive resources lie unused, while the human needs that they could satisfy are not met.[1]

1. Since this book may be read by young people, it may be necess-

To end this, Soviet communism developed a series of plans, starting in 1928, the purpose of which broadly was to estimate accurately the extent of human needs in U.S.S.R., to assess their importance, to calculate how far they could be supplied within the limitations of existing resources, to organise production to meet those needs on an expanding scale, and to repeat this process every five years so as to ensure that production was nationally controlled and maintained always at the highest possible level.

There can be little doubt that the Soviet Union has greatly improved the industrial production of the country. Unfortunately it is difficult to measure this achievement. For one thing, a substantial part of the production has been for military purposes. The Soviet leaders judged this to be imposed upon them by world conditions, and in the light of Hitler's attack upon them in 1941 this judgment was largely vindicated so far as it relates to the period before the War. Even apart from military needs the government of the U.S.S.R. has chosen to direct a great part of the economic effort of their people to the production of capital equipment. The production of goods for immediate use has for this reason been severely curtailed and the standard of living enjoyed by the people has remained low by Western standards. The

ary to explain that there have been many years in which chronic unemployment prevailed, e.g. in the building industry, while people lived in cramped and squalid houses from which they longed to escape —people who were able and willing to work hard to achieve this. More spectacular even was the actual burning of wheat and coffee and destruction of 'surplus' livestock, while people went ill-nourished to the point of suffering. It should be noted that these desperate measures were not undertaken by callous men, but by men of undoubted humanity like President F. D. Roosevelt in his attempt to keep the enormously productive American economy from total collapse, in 1932 and the following years. The slump had begun in 1929, but for more than two years the leaders of America had found no way of arresting its progress to more and more disastrous levels.

people have constantly been urged to forgo present satis-
factions in the expectation of a good time coming, when the
foundations will have been securely laid for mass production
in the great factories and farms. The whole process was
hampered from the beginning by the devastations of the
First World War and the long and bitter civil war which
followed, as well as by the low level of industrial development and general and technical education which the Soviets
inherited from Czardom. A further tremendous setback was
the German invasion of the Second World War, resulting in
the destruction, partial or complete, of many important
industrial plants in the greatest centres of ore and coal
mining, engineering and petroleum production, and a huge
loss of agricultural stock and machinery. In these circumstances, and for other reasons, comparison between the Soviet
system and other systems in periods of capital accumulation
and basic economic development are almost impossible. But
in spite of all difficulties of measurement, it cannot be gainsaid
that the adoption of a planned economy in Russia has made
an immense impact on the world, and has played an important part in accelerating the adoption of planning in other
countries, and indeed internationally. The moral and political conditions of such planning and the scope of the plans
are greatly varied. In capitalist America there is the planning
of the economy of a particular region as in the Tennessee
Valley Authority: in Britain the planning of particular
sectors of industry by national boards (railways, mining, gas
and electricity). There are also the comprehensive plans for
European recovery which Secretary Marshall initiated.
Governmental intervention in the direction of the economic
process, in one form or another, is now well established all
over the Western world, which has already ceased, therefore,
to be in the old sense a world of capitalist 'free' enterprise.
It is precisely in respect of this element of freedom that the

Soviet conception of planning and economic progress is most sharply criticised. Such has been the preoccupation with statistical and economic measurement of progress, such the rigour of the planning, such the pressure for quick and striking vindication of the communist theories, that the power of government and party have been used relentlessly against all opposing or merely recalcitrant elements. As in the worst phases of capitalism, men have been valued only as 'producers', and their status as moral personalities has been taken from them. The necessities of the plans have contributed towards such a growth of state power over the life of the individual as has never been experienced in history.

(2) *Social justice.* Communism aims at a classless, i.e. an equalitarian society, for where there are measurable differences in standard of life, social stratification will follow, and classes will form, seeking to defend and to enhance their privileges. An early Bolshevik version of equalitarian theory provided the same level of remuneration for the high government officer and the humble working man. As a corollary of this, responsibility was to be shared equally too, extreme developments of self-government in factory, army, school, even in prison, and of course in all municipal and state affairs, were contemplated and, in a limited way, attempted.

These equalitarian visions were soon dissipated in contact with the realities of life. There has of course been an enormous upset of social relations. New men have come to the top, women have entered upon new opportunities without limit, the great hereditary wealth of landlord and capitalist has become a common property. But in the remuneration of different grades of work wide differences are now established. These differences correspond broadly to those with which we are familiar. Highly trained specialists get more than skilled men, skilled get more than unskilled, energetic piece-workers get high wages, popular artists and entertainers

[42]

get immoderate rewards in money or special privileges. Well placed men are able to get advantages for their children. Education, health and other social services have been developed to supplement individual earnings, and play a part in mitigating inequalities. Advancement has come to depend too upon conformity with the prevailing opinions of the 'Party', and unquestioning subservience to authority. At the other extreme, those who have conspicuously failed to conform have been deprived of all rights—the right to citizenship, the right to food rations, the right to family life. They have been sent to work camps, frequently in the more inhospitable parts of the vast Soviet territory, and used up, toiling in conditions of savage harshness, on some project necessary to the execution of the five year plans. It should, however, be noted that these grimmer aspects of life in the Soviet Union are fully compatible with an existence for the ordinary man or woman, not much bothering about ideas or about his fellowmen, in which opportunity and hope of improvement are real and fairly secure.

The régime, so far as it rests upon popular support or consent, is, therefore, well established, and by various well planned measures is always able to secure an overwhelming support for itself at elections. No party other than the highly centralised, highly disciplined Communist Party, is allowed to exist. Non-members are included in the lists of candidates presented to the electors for approval or rejection. (There are no alternative candidates.) But no non-communists can organise themselves to present a programme different from that of the government and Party, or associate themselves as a distinct group. The differences of opinion, and conflicts of ambition that are natural to men at all times and in all places do not on that account cease to exist, or to express themselves. In the Soviet Union, they must do so within the Communist Party. The full meaning of this does not at first appear. It is

D   [43]

sometimes represented to us by Communists that within the Party discussion is full and free, that the spirit and constitution of the Communist Party are democratic in the most complete degree. Yet many who have for some time been members of the Party have found the moral atmosphere stifling to the personality. They have found themselves in a minority, forced to accept the majority decision abjectly, or to be suspected, watched, degraded or expelled. This arises from the principle that the Party must present a monolithic unity to the outside world. No member finding himself in a minority, may appeal beyond the Party to the support of the wider public. It was one of the inexcusable political sins of Trotsky that at one stage, baffled by Stalin's control of the Party, he tried to do this.

The consequence of this organisation is inevitable. The only hope of a minority lies in *conspiracy*, in underground secret preparation to overthrow by force and by surprise the dominant group in the Party. Hence the amazing fact that by 1939 all the Old Guard of the Bolshevik Party had perished in unsuccessful attempts to overthrow the power of Stalin. Hence the bewildering series of trials which between 1934 and 1938 took place in Moscow, by means of which (together with summary execution of many others) all opposition to Stalin within the Party and the army was for the time suppressed. Hence also the continuing need for a special and large-scale organisation of secret police, functioning within all the organs of state and within the Party itself, as the watchful protector of the régime, acting right outside the system of law, dependent only upon the personal authority of the dictator.

A remarkable feature of these trials in the years before the war was the regularity with which men of undoubted capacity and courage, who had been bitterly opposed to Stalin's power and policies, confessed their guilt and acknowledged themselves to have been shamefully misguided in the courses they had taken. To the Western democratic world their behaviour was incomprehensible, and recourse was had to explanations in terms of torture and drugs.

Such means were in fact employed to break the wills of the accused persons.[1] But it seems certain that because the conspirators were genuine Communists, who really accepted the Bolshevik conception of the monolithic Communist Party, they were in fact forced by the logic of their own principles to acknowledge that Stalin was right. To offer determined opposition to Stalin they would have had to escape from the rigidity of Marxist and Leninist teaching. In other words the harsh discipline of the Communist by his Party is of the very essence of Communist teaching. It is a system that destroys freedom, destroys the individual.

1. See, e.g., *Conspiracy of Silence*, by Alexander Weissberg, Hamish Hamilton, 1952.

VI

Communism, Religion and Morality

WE have seen already that Marx was a materialist before he was a communist. He thought religion to be untrue. In his thinking, matter is self-existent, there is no God. This is an essential part of Marxist communism.

Communist Theories about Religion. The question remains for the Marxist. How is the prevalence and the undoubted importance of religion in human history to be accounted for? The answer given is in two parts:

(1) Religion for the Marxist is a survival from the immaturity of the human race. When men do not know how to interpret nature by scientific observation and experiment, they tend to imagine the change and movement in nature as being due to the activity of beings having at least some of the attributes of personality (animism, anthropomorphism). The approach of men to nature, and especially to what seems powerful or important in nature, is therefore made by way of prayer, offerings or the fulfilment of such conditions as seem likely to win the favour, or perhaps appease the anger, of the gods. In principle, according to Marxist views, science supersedes religion, substituting positive, verified knowledge of nature's laws for the imagination and speculation that were the only resource of men before science enabled them to understand and to control their environment in nature.

(2) But besides this, Marxist theory explains religion as having existed to meet certain important psychological and social needs of men. To sustain their courage in face of danger and disaster, to secure unity and cohesion among men in society, to console them, frustrated as they often are in their

dearest hopes in life, and always finally by death, men have created a world of imagination to transform the real world.

Such naturalistic ways of accounting for the existence and persistence of religion are not specially Marxist. Some forms of naturalism, while agreeing with Marxism in refusing to accept religion as *true*, have nevertheless considered its influence upon human life to be valuable and have even believed that religion is *necessary* to sustain society, culture and a civilised life. The Marxist, however, regards religion as a necessity in modern times *only in a class society*. In such a society, where some are exploited by others more powerful, religion offers to the poor and propertyless some satisfaction in hopes of heaven for present earthly miseries. Also, the ruling class in such a society willingly believes that its own privileges are deserved and represents all opposition to its power as rebellion against the will of God. This makes religion an instrument of exploitation. It is branded by Marx as an 'opiate of the people', belonging to the period of proletarian ignorance and impotence. In the classless society religion (it is thought) will have no functions of this sort, and will die out. So long as men are without science they turn to the medicine man and the priest. So long as they turn to these they will continue to neglect the means of self-help through science and social organisation. In the interests of human progress, therefore, religion must be attacked and destroyed. The proletarian must learn that the Church is his enemy, the enemy of his class, belonging to the forces of social reaction, opposed to the revolution.

Communism and Morality. The Marxist conception of morality seems to involve just as radical rejection of morality as of religion.

In Plato's *Republic* one of the speakers, Thrasymachus, defends the view that 'Justice is the interest of the stronger'. By this he means that those who are powerful and privileged ('the ruling class') have an interest in maintaining society in its existing form, as a 'going concern'. To them, the conduct that assists this is good. They, therefore, encourage honesty, temperance, respect for the rights of property, bravery in war defending or extending their own society's wealth and power, and so on. Such qualities of character are praised as virtues. Marx and Lenin seem sometimes to adopt this view, and for them, of course, the 'virtues' that sustain a class society become obstacles to the overthrow of that society. The morality that serves to maintain the state of bourgeois or capitalist domination has, they contend, no force of obligation for the proletarian.

At times, therefore, the Marxist speaks as if the whole concept of virtue had no validity. He encourages a cynical and contemptuous attitude to general ethical principles, abstract ideals of virtue, moral law. By appeal to these, he contends, the workers have been kept in subjection. Morality takes on the colour of a bourgeois concept; the disillusioned proletarian must throw it aside, and adopt for himself whatever ideas and policies and conduct will destroy the exploiters' power, and serve the revolution.

At the same time, the Marxist has a way of condemning capitalism and the capitalist as if on moral grounds. He seems sometimes to *blame* the exploiter as if he regarded exploitation as not only offensive to the exploited, but *immoral*. Again the classless society might be thought to commend itself not only as economically more stable and productive, but as morally more satisfactory. This moral appeal is, however, implicit only in communism. Apparently communism relies on the self interest of the individual proletarian. His 'solidarity' with his own class, before, during and after the revolution, is assumed to be the solidarity of a common self interest. The relations of mutual trust that are necessary to conspirators if they are to succeed, the reliability of the citizen in the classless society afterwards, are supposed to owe nothing to any sense of moral obligation. Even so, it is anticipated in orthodox communist doctrine that the mutual comradeship of the citizens will be such as to make the coercive power of the State superfluous. The State, which in the judgment of the Marxist is essentially an instrument of class power, will necessarily, as the classless society is securely established, 'wither away'.

The Consequence of these Views. It is difficult to believe that Communism does not owe a great deal of its progress in the modern world to the very morality that it theoretically denies and rejects. Not a few of the 'comrades' have been willing to sacrifice themselves for *the cause*, the triumph of which they could not themselves enjoy. Some of them have belonged to the middle class and have identified themselves with the proletariat out of a sense of the justice of proletarian claims, or at least in protest against the manifest injustice of exploitation.

In spite of this, Communism insists on excluding all moral concepts from its interpretation of man. This, of course, is consistent with its basic materialism. For Marxism, man exists as a member of a biological species; man exists also as a member of a particular ethnic or cultural group (Negro, Englishman, Slav, etc.); above all, he exists as a member of a class defined in economic terms (proletarian, peasant, bourgeois, etc.) *As a moral personality*, having an inward life of aspiration, anxiety, guilt, repentance, a consciousness of relationship across all divisions of class and nationality with other men who have themselves their own inward depth of thought and feeling, *man may be said to have no existence for Marxism.*

So when the individual human being gets in the way of the Party's programme, he becomes quite simply a class enemy. Hence the completeness with which Communism subordinates human personal interests of all kinds to the exigencies of its economic programme; and even within the economic field, man the producer swamps man the consumer. This preoccupation with *production* is, of course, partly to be explained by the tremendous problems of production facing the Communist countries in the early stages of industrialisation. But the neglect of the consumer interest must also be attributed in part to the lack of any evaluation in Marxism of the *ends* of human life. Marxism is preoccupied with the *means* of life, and strictly speaking knows nothing about any ends that are above or distinct from the process of living itself.[1]

While this may justly be charged against Marxist theory and Communist practice as dominated by that theory, it should not be forgotten that few men and women, even among Communists, can be exhaustively described in terms of their politics. Personal ambition, love and friendship, sporting, artistic and scientific interests, local custom and personal traits, suggest ends of life to the Communist as to other men. Moral conviction and enthusiasm have played a great part in the history of modern communism and account considerably for its advance. The authority of Lenin was partly the authority of a man of consistent character. Many are certainly attracted to Communism by the broad justice of its economic programme, and the moral earnestness and invincible purposefulness of its supporters. The example of Douglas Hyde,[2] a lay preacher who joined the Communist Party because it seemed to be uncompromisingly committed

1. It is, of course, lamentably true that there have been periods when 'making money' (significant only as a *means*) became the dominant purpose of society in Great Britain and America, and the true *ends* of human life were largely ignored, and often outraged and violated. But in Christianity we had the means of knowing we were doing wrong.
2. See his autobiography *I Believed.*

to champion the disinherited, is by no means singular. Men of that stamp, earnestly concerned to be seriously committed to a worthy purpose in life, are attracted by something in Communism (and, it must be acknowledged, repelled by the absence, or seeming absence, of a similar integrity of purpose in Western democracy). A number of such recruits to Marxism have been later dismayed by an inhuman hardness in their associates. They have found that the methods of the Party involve them in obedience to authoritative direction from the centre against their own convictions, to the point of losing their personal integrity. Conformity to the Party line has required from them a surrender of judgment and freedom which reduces their humanity to automatism. This characteristic tragedy of the thoughtful communist has been exposed for us repeatedly in books such as *The God that Failed, Truth will Out, Darkness at Noon*, and others. The theoretical denial of the validity of morality bears bitter fruit in a practical disregard for the basic moral need of men to be themselves. To have any substantial degree of freedom of decision a Communist must be one of the central group that plans and pronounces. Rivalry, mistrust, scheming develop out of these circumstances. Beneath the surface of unity presented to the outer world as we have already seen there have existed at most times in the history of the Communist Party throughout this century, bitter divisions, engendering suspicion, hatred and fear. Time and again, where circumstances permitted, these have resulted in violent death. One of the most terrible features of Communism has been the number of its most notable leaders who have perished at the hands, or by the orders, of their former close confederates, branded as traitors, and pitilessly destroyed with every mark of ignominy.[1]

1. In any final assessment of Communism in respect of its moral outlook, allowance must be made for the special conditions of revolu-

The only test of conduct by Marxist standards concerns the degree to which that conduct aids or opposes the Communist Party in its revolutionary struggle, or in its 'socialist construction' after the revolution is accomplished. This test is applied not only to conduct, but to artistic work, and even to scientific theory. The moral life, art, the sciences, are not regarded as having a significance of their own apart from their social effects. They are not allowed to develop according to their own interests and laws. Free exploration and free criticism in these fields are heavily discouraged. Official Marxist-Leninist-Stalinist doctrines or standards are from time to time promulgated in an article in *Pravda*, or by resolution of the central organs of the Party at the instigation of a leading Party man. These decisions have sometimes been made effective by the dismissal, or threatened dismissal or disgrace (or, it may be, even imprisonment or execution) of outstanding scientists, musicians or men of letters; rivals, who may be men of obviously inferior gifts, but conformists, accepting and trumpeting the approved view, replace those who have failed to observe the Party line.

The Tactical Flexibility of Communism in Religious Matters. Tactical changes of emphasis in all these matters are common, and even in regard to religion the rigidity of the Marxist theoretical position allows for co-operation, for temporary advantage, between the Communist Party and Church organisations. On certain particular questions, for limited periods, the aims of churchman and communist may coincide. Examples are, the desire of both Christian and Communist to prevent the outbreak of war in Europe in 1951: or in an African territory, support of a threatened native interest

tion and post-revolution. The prosecution of war involves divergence from the standards of peace-time life. The Communists take themselves to be in the position of conducting war operations against actual or potential enemies.

against a white government policy. In Hungary after the war the new Communist government sought to secure popular favour, or it may be to confuse its opponents, by spending money on the repair of damaged churches.[3] In the Soviet Union itself, in consideration of the unqualified support offered by the Church authorities to the war effort, and as part of the policy of uniting all elements of the population by an appeal to the past history of the Russian peoples, the Church was ostentatiously given public recognition in a new agreement with the State. Always, these are merely tactical arrangements, recognising the *de facto* strength of religious interests, or seeking to exploit or at least to neutralise them, in the struggle for Communist power. They do not alter the basic hostility of Marxism to religion itself, and to the churches. In the 'liberalised' Stalin Constitution of the U.S.S.R. (1936), the Church was given legal freedom of *worship*, the atheist movement was given freedom of *propaganda*. This confirmed, in a formula that may have a ring of impartiality, a position that, of course, in practice favours the anti-religious Communist Party. Freedom of worship does not mean freedom to propagate by speech or writing, to organise schools or missions, and to teach the young. It means not much more than freedom to hold Church services and to practise the religious life within one's own home. By contrast, the Communist Party with its hands on the state machine at all levels of authority, has power to shape the whole educational system, and unlimited opportunity by press and radio and film and public meeting to present its atheist philosophy.

Communism as a secular substitute for Religion. It becomes clear that the Communist Party functions in the Soviet

3. These benefits were never unconditionally bestowed: they involved in some degree the surrender of control of appointments to Communist-dominated state organs.

Union as a secular equivalent of an established church in a Christian country. It forms an élite of leadership, carefully selected, thoroughly trained, severely disciplined and highly organised. Its role is not only within the State, but alongside it, or even above it, in the sense that it defines the purposes, and decides the policies which the State then executes. The Party is like the Church of the Middle Ages, providing the fundamental teaching, supplying also the well indoctrinated personnel to the leading positions in the State, and working in close partnership with the State to secure the prevalence of certain beliefs and certain patterns of life in the community.

In respect of the psychology of Communism this analogy goes far. The writings of Marx and Lenin, until lately also of Stalin, have the authority of sacred scriptures: Stalin's role as interpreter of communist orthodoxy was latterly like that of a pope rather than a secular ruler, although he combined both functions. The honour and obedience offered to Stalin in his later years were expressed in the language of religious devotion, as to the vicegerent of God. Lenin's tomb, in the Red Square of Moscow, containing his embalmed remains, became a shrine, a place of quasi-religious pilgrimage. Communism has in fact evolved into a 'secular religion', a movement without God indeed, but expressing and inculcating a total attitude to life, and seeking to assert itself as a comprehensive authoritative guide over the whole of human interest and endeavour. Marxist communism when it achieves state power becomes *totalitarian*, suppressing with more or less energy and efficiency every dissident opinion, and offering itself as a sufficient foundation for a new civilisation.

It is, therefore, a mistaken view which thinks of Communism in terms of the political parties of a democracy. Within the context of Western political life, the Communist Party may be forced to operate much like other parties, and can easily be mistaken for such. But it has a larger scope than our political parties. It would be nearer the truth to think of the Communist Party as a secularised rival to the Church, seeking to do for a new civilisation what the Church did for Christendom.

The autobiography of communists frequently discloses that Marxism, its element of utopian vision, its sense of co-operating in the majestic dialectic of historical development, has given to them a significant purpose to which to commit themselves, a firm dogmatic basis for the ordering of their thought, and a concrete authority to trust, supporting and supplementing their own incompleteness. The scientists who have become communists often claim that Marxism is simply science applied to society, and for some scientists there is no doubt a special fascination in the social planning and conditioning of men's minds that it involves. But the attitude of these scientists to Marxist philosophy, to the Party, to the Soviet Union, is not the experimental attitude that they exhibit towards a scientific theory or a scientific institution. It is an attitude of faith, of personal commitment, a religious attitude. They have never held Christian faith, or have abandoned it. Into this vacuum in their souls has come Marxism, congenial to the special bias of their minds as scientists in certain ways, and playing in their lives the part of a substitute religion.

Similarly, in Germany between the great wars, a population that had partly abandoned Christianity committed itself to an ostensibly political movement, National Socialism, which however turned out to have the characteristics of a revived twentieth-century tribal religion. These two movements, nazism and communism, unlike in many things, have this general feature in common. *Their rise and growth in the twentieth century is an indication not only of the economic and political crises, but, more significantly, of the spiritual crisis of our time.*

VII

The Post-War Expansion of World Communism

THIS book is not a history of Communism, and no attempt is being made in it to show how, from its first success in Russia, the Communist Party has achieved control of the government of other countries, viz. Poland, East Germany, Czechoslovakia, Rumania, Hungary, Bulgaria, the Baltic countries of Lithuania, Estonia and Latvia, now incorporated in the U.S.S.R., Yugoslavia and China. In all these, except China, the achievement of power by the Communist Party was due directly or indirectly to the support of the Soviet Red Army. All of them except Yugoslavia and perhaps China have been very closely bound into the economic, military and political system that is dominated by the Communist Party and government of the U.S.S.R. A conspicuous proof of this was given in 1948 when the American Secretary of State, Mr George Marshall, offered economic aid to the countries affected by the war. Poland and Czechoslovakia at first indicated willingness to accept this aid, and then, on instructions from the U.S.S.R., withdrew from participation, and proceeded to dovetail their industrial and commercial planning with that of the Soviet Union. Many other illustrations of the same sort could be given, but the most striking is provided by the expulsion of Yugoslavia from the confraternity of communist states in 1949.

Yugoslavia had become communist by rapid stages after the war of 1939-45, under the leadership of Tito, a Moscow-trained Serbian communist, who had served the Comintern abroad as well as in his own country. During the war, his organisation of guerrilla forces was countenanced, and later firmly supported, by the British government and armed forces, in the belief that Tito's guerrillas were vigorously attacking the German occupying armies. This war-time contact with the West, and the knowledge that such contact could be resumed, encouraged Tito, a man of independent and ambitious character, to resist the attempt of the Soviet power to dominate and control the development of communist Yugoslavia. This control was exercised in various ways, all designed to ensure that in relations between the U.S.S.R. and other Communist countries, the interests of the Soviet Union should be paramount. The outward expression of this situation was the organisation known as the Cominform, which besides the Communist Parties of the East European communist States, included also those of France and Italy. When Tito resisted Russian pressure and attempted to initiate and sustain independent relations with other Balkan governments, he was denounced by the Cominform, and Yugoslavia was expelled from its membership.

While remaining firmly attached to Marxist theory and Leninist practice within Yugoslavia, his government has established and continues to maintain independent relations with the states of the non-communist world, and has accepted economic aid from Britain and the United States of America, and even entered into military alliance with Greece and Turkey for mutual support vis-à-vis the threatening power of the U.S.S.R.

Tito's resistance possibly expressed primarily the unwillingness of an able, self reliant and ambitious man to be dominated by other men. It expressed also the national sentiment, the sense of independent historical existence, of Yugoslavia, even of communist Yugoslavs, and to this national sentiment Tito could make appeal in calling for the sacrifices necessary to make an independent policy effective. It is certain that exactly similar situations arose in all of the satellite Communist Parties and governments of Eastern Europe, except that they were not favourably placed to receive the support of the West in offering resistance. The leading communists of these countries suspected of 'Titoist' tendencies were, therefore, 'liquidated' without too much difficulty; that is to say, they were removed from office, degraded, imprisoned or executed according to the degree of the danger to Soviet dominance they represented.[1]

Chinese Communism. More portentous for the future is the fact that in 1949 China, home of the most ancient civilisation and the most numerous people of the world, came firmly under the control of a communist government. There are some features of quite special interest in this Chinese Communist Revolution.

Like Russia at the time of the Revolution, China is a nation of peasants. At the very least 80 per cent of the population lives on the land, mostly as tenants of very small farms, intensively cultivated but capable for the most part of yielding only a modest, and even a meagre living, by the methods employed. The urban proletariat, properly so called (that is wage-earning workers organised for production in large factories, mines, railway systems), was relatively small in numbers, and capitalist industry was at an early stage in its development.

The Chinese Communist Party (founded in 1921) at first (guided by Marx's teaching and the Russian example) assumed that it would be in the towns and from proletarians that it would draw its strength, and achieve revolutionary success and the seizure of power. Throughout the period from 1923 to 1935, the official policy of communism in

1. The powerful reform of Communism under Gomulka in Poland, and the similar unsuccessful attempt of the Hungarians under Nagy in the autumn of 1956 show the reality of the opposition to Soviet control even of the Communist Parties of other nations.

relation to China was based on the hope of urban insurrection under Communist Party leadership. A succession of leaders appointed by the Comintern to carry out this policy failed to make headway. Meantime, Mao Tse-tung, a convinced Marxist, eager to learn all that the Russians had to teach, had been forced by circumstances into dependence on a military force composed mainly of peasants, operating in the country-side and incapable of holding any large town against the superior armies of Chiang Kai-shek, who from 1927 held supreme governmental authority in the greater part of China. Out of his experience in the attempt to establish areas in Central China as Chinese Soviets, Mao drew conclusions regarding the conditions of success for communism as follows:

(1) The Communist Party must find a 'mass base' in the poorer peasantry.

(2) The Party itself must maintain its cohesion and strength by a vigorous discipline and doctrine (Leninist democratic centralism).

(3) It must recruit (mainly from the peasantry) and train under reliable party leadership a strong Red Army.

(4) It must gain control of an area strategically located (capable of defence and from which in favourable circum-stances it might extend its power).

(5) This area must be economically self-sufficient.

To fulfil these conditions, adapting Marxist theory to the conditions of China, Mao Tse-tung set out from Central China with some 60,000 of an army on a march to the north-west province of Yenan. This epic journey of several thousand miles was accomplished, not without heavy loss, and under Mao's leadership in this remote region an agrarian-military soviet system was established in 1935.

Mao gained this success with the peasants by uniting the poorer and middle peasants and even some occupying bigger farms, against the richer farmers and landowners. The land was more equally distributed but left in private (family) possession. This was a reformist rather than a revolutionary programme: other elements in it were the beginnings of a popular system of education, and the establishment of good government, free of corruption under the leadership of the Party and of the Red Army, themselves well disciplined bodies, sustained by a strong sense of mission as the pioneers of a new China. The relatively small number of Western visitors to the area controlled by the Communists in the years following 1935, were much impressed by the moderation and efficiency of the régime and by the evidence of positive support for it among the people.

During the next ten years, the strategy of communism in China was conditioned by the fact that Japan was conducting an aggressive war on China. Based on Manchuria (occupied in 1934), the Japanese expanded their attack by stages southwards, occupying the cities and main lines of communication between them. The policy of Mao Tse-tung was to co-operate with the National Government of Chiang Kai-shek in opposing the Japanese, while maintaining in his own area a distinct governmental and military organisation, controlled by the Communist Party. On this basis the Communists were able to extend the area of their control by winning back from the Japanese large tracts of country outside the bigger cities. Not only so; but by emphasising the three principles of Sun Yat Sen (national freedom, democracy and people's welfare) in the somewhat vague form he had given them, they attracted into sympathetic collaboration with them many liberal-minded Chinese who were becoming distrustful of the heterogeneous and somewhat corrupt Kuomintang, the Nationalist Party of Chiang Kai-shek.

Supplied with the arms of the Japanese Manchurian armies, surrendered to the Soviet Army at the end of the war in 1945, the Chinese Communists soon found themselves in a favourable position to challenge the power of Chiang Kai-shek, who seemed determined in turn to destroy communism as the necessary preliminary to the security of his own authority.

Although the Nationalist Army was numerically much stronger, and generally better equipped, the leadership and morale of the Communist proved superior, and in 1948 and 1949, it succeeded in gaining control of all mainland China. Chiang Kai-shek retreated with the remains of his army to Formosa.

In the years that followed, Mao Tse-tung showed himself a thoroughgoing follower of the communism not only of Marx and Lenin, but of Stalin. He has not subordinated himself to the directions of Moscow, but he has followed with Chinese variations the same methods and policies. Making allowance for the difference of circumstances, there are to be found in Chinese communism:

(1) something corresponding to the N.E.P.;

(2) the use of terror. A favourite form in China has been the 'trial' of political offenders by mobs under Communist leadership;

(3) the use of political prisoners in vast numbers on works of a particularly arduous kind, like flood control or railway building;

(4) the development of heavy industry as the basis of military and industrial power, rapidly and ruthlessly;

(5) severe censorship of publication, exclusive control of propaganda, Communist monopoly of education and the expulsion of all rival ideologies, notably the missionaries of the Christian churches;

(6) the reorganisation of agriculture in two stages with a view to eliminating private property and private enterprise in farming, under increasing pressure from the Communist Party;

(7) the building up of military strength and the support,

direct or indirect, of Communist Parties of neighbouring countries by this means.

The Chinese participated on a great scale in the Korean War, and are thought to have given substantial help and guidance to the communists in Indo-China.

The one striking difference between the Communist Party of China and that of the U.S.S.R. so far has been the absence of internecine strife and the liquidation of deviationists. Mao Tse-tung occupies a position more like that of Lenin than of Stalin and he has not provoked the struggles against his authority that led Stalin to the savage purgations of the Party in defence of his own absolute power over it.

The Chinese programme of communist industrial planning can be carried out only with the help of the much more advanced production of the U.S.S.R. and the satellite states of Eastern Europe. This makes China dependent on the U.S.S.R. and the Communist Party of China naturally looks to the more experienced Party of the Soviet Union for guidance. Chinese go to the U.S.S.R. for training and many Russian technical advisers are at work in China. But there seems to be more fundamental equality in the relations of China to the Soviet Union than between Russia and any other Communist country. Common interest meantime holds them together; but there are possibilities of acute rivalry in two fields, (i) in the control of territories like Sinkiang and Manchuria in which both have strong interests not necessarily identical, and (ii) in the control of communist parties in other Asian countries such as Burma, Japan, Indonesia, India, Malaya.

The size of China, the independent nature of Chinese evolution and its potential rank as a great power, e.g. as a member of the Security Council of the United Nations, make it certain that China will not be a mere instrument of Soviet policy.

VIII

The Communist Party in Britain

IN timber country where tens of thousands of trees, felled and trimmed up river, are floated to the big mills downstream to be sawn or pulped, it sometimes happens that they jam, and pile up dangerously. The expert lumberman is able to judge the time and place at which, by levering here and there, his own strength can so upset the balance of mighty forces that movement is restored, and the river, flowing on, carries with it the huge mass of timber to the chosen place where it will finally be diverted to the sawmills.

It is a picture like this that comes to mind in contemplating the achievement of the Communist Party in the present century. A relatively tiny body of men in several countries, by adroit and resolute application of their ideas and energies at the right times and places, have been able to give direction to immense social forces. The lumberman needs a suitable instrument, a rigid wieldy bar of steel, and the knowledge to use it at the point where the logs are locked, and then the momentum of river and timber does the rest. The leaders of Communism, taught by Lenin, have forged in the Party an instrument, rigid in its discipline and completely under their control, to guide vast numbers of men and exploit their energies for purposes chosen by the Communist central leadership. This is most strikingly illustrated by China, where perhaps 600,000,000 men and women find themselves, without much understanding or choice, under the iron control of the few around Mao Tse-tung who give orders through an obedient Communist Party.

'*The Communist Technique in Britain*'. It is the constant

endeavour of the Communists to achieve similar results in Britain by methods suitably adapted to British conditions. Their success cannot be measured by their poor showing in elections for Parliament or city councils. In these elections they have had to obey the British electoral laws, abide by democratic procedures, explain their policy in public, and accept the verdict of the secret ballot with a majority of ordinary citizens exercising their voting rights. In these conditions the Communist Party has suffered repeated and ignominious defeat. It has been too obvious that their programme is designed not to meet the needs of the British people, but to conform to the 'general line' of international communism, dictated by far-off Moscow.

The influence of the Party in Britain has been restricted in the political field by the continued refusal of the Labour Party to permit any alliance or working agreement with Communism. This has been of crucial importance: in politics the Communist Party has had to stand on its own feet, and it has wobbled badly.

But on the industrial front the picture is very different. A few trade unions forbid the holding of office in them by Communists, but for the most part it is possible for Communists to play their part in trade union organisation without restriction. They have so far succeeded in taking advantage of this opportunity that they have gained substantial control in a number of important unions, and occupy leading positions in many more.

How they achieve this is well worthy of study. The methods are clearly set forth in a book by Bob Darke called *The Communist Technique in Britain*,[1] written after leaving the Party which he had served faithfully and successfully as an active trade unionist for many years.

The basic unit of Communist organisation is the 'fraction'.

1. Originally published by Collins 1953 and printed later as a Penguin.

A 'fraction' may be set up in any context: in a block of flats, to agitate and lead the tenants in a strike against increased rents; among homeless people to incite and lead them to 'squat' in empty west-end flats, in a bus depot, a small factory, a department of a large factory, a trade union branch, a branch of a professional association, of a dramatic club, of the Anglo-Soviet Friendship Society, of a Peace Society. The 'fraction' consists of the Communist Party members who are also members of the group in question. It meets to apply the general line of the Party within that group, to decide on tactics and allocate duties to each Party member in executing them. The 'fraction' does not act independently. It acts on instructions from someone appointed for the purpose by the Central Committee of the Communist Party of Great Britain, and must submit regular reports on its work to this authority. The fraction is commissioned to influence to the greatest possible extent the action or policy of the group in which it operates, so as to promote the ideas and the power of Communism. By careful study of its opportunities, and resolute united action, a small fraction may succeed surprisingly in doing this.

In trade unions, to quote Bob Darke, 'branch membership may be large, but attendance at branch meetings is invariably small.[1] This lack of interest on the part of the average trade unionist is the Communist's big opportunity. He will pack a thinly attended meeting with his own comrades and his sympathisers, he will ease Party members into the chair, on to the Committee. . . . In my own time I have eased through Communist-inspired resolutions on peace, on Korea, on Russia, long after the fixed time for union business to end.

1. A figure recently quoted indicates a less than 5 per cent attendance of members as a usual proportion for branch meetings of the A.E.U. in Lanarkshire. (See Article by John Robertson in *Scio News*, December, 1956.)

I have eased through these resolutions knowing that the men who might have opposed them and defeated them have looked at the clock and gone home.' To give some idea of the numbers involved, in a factory of 2,000 workers, a Communist fraction of only 30 has succeeded in securing the election of six of its own men out of a total of twelve shop stewards.

The effectiveness of Communist action is easily misjudged by our tendency to apply wrong tests. Take as an example an industrial dispute arising out of the principle of the 'closed shop'. This principle (by no means universally applied) is that no one should be employed by a particular industrial undertaking who is not a member of the appropriate trade union. It has sometimes happened that a single worker for some reason has resigned from the union, or has broken the rules and been expelled. The workman is a good craftsman and productive worker and the firm wishes to retain him. How far in a case like this is it reasonable for a union to go in enforcing the closed shop principle, compelling the management to dismiss the man, or the man himself to accept union membership and abide by union rules? Responsible trade union officials will act in such a situation with deliberation and prudence. They will act within any existing agreement with the employers. They are unwilling to jeopardise such an agreement, probably the result of prolonged negotiation, by any rash action. They are unwilling also to involve their members in loss of wages by striking. They are acting on the basis that trade unionism is part of the continuing industrial life of this country. *They wish to maintain our industry as a going concern within which the power of the trade unions will continue to be used to enhance the standard of living of their members.* Any sacrifice they ask their members to make must be related to a more or less immediate and measurable gain they hope to achieve.

To the Communist the position is far otherwise. He has always in his mind the conviction that the revolution will develop *out of the breakdown* of the existing system. Possibly he may have in view some more limited hope, for example, that a hold up in the British aircraft industry will be to the military advantage of the Communist countries. He will be satisfied therefore if he can succeed in stirring up trouble, and still more satisfied if he can cause it to spread. By cunning presentation of the case he can sometimes gain support for an unofficial strike, which, if they are not to lose influence over the workers, the official trade union leaders may be forced to recognise and approve. Tempers may rise and the employers be provoked into some unwise course or summary action. After weeks of confused discussion, the strike may end in a compromise, or in complete failure as regards its original ostensible object. If perchance there is a strong reaction against the ring-leaders, it may not seriously affect the Communist Party, because the Party as such has never been brought in. Any discredited member of the 'fraction' which has secretly planned and guided the whole episode, can be withdrawn and sent away to carry on his work in another place, and the 'fraction' itself will be re-organised and live to fight another day. If the strike is successful of course full credit is claimed for the Communist leadership. In any case, industrial output has been reduced, confusion has been created in industrial relationships, official union leadership has been embarrassed by having to follow rather than lead. It may be one or two new militant workers have been discovered and brought into contact with the Communist Party. They will be followed up and cultivated with a view to committed membership and thorough indoctrination. All this, from the point of view of Communism, is great gain.

The trade union movement in Britain derives its main

importance from its bargaining function. Wages and working conditions for industrial and commercial workers and
salaried staff are nowadays governed for most people by
national agreements hammered out between executive bodies
representing on the one hand the employed and on the other
the employers in a particular industry or craft or profession.
But besides this work, trade unions meet *with each other* to
discuss matters of common interest and to promote purposes
in the national life which are common to them all. For these
purposes most trade unions in Britain are affiliated to the
Labour Party, to whose funds they contribute by dues levied
on their members.[1] For this reason trade unions are represented at the annual policy-making conference of the Labour
Party, and their delegates carry with them the immense
voting power of their unions. It is customary for these
delegates to be instructed how they are to vote on important
matters, by the unions they represent. This means that the
unions, *in which Communists may be very active*, meet to discuss
these matters in their branches before the Conference, and to
frame resolutions for the guidance of their delegates. Here
is an opportunity for the Communists, who are excluded
from personal participation in the Conference of the Labour
Party, to influence its deliberations through the unions.
Every year resolutions, advocating more or less in disguise
the Communist Party line, are submitted and discussed at
the Labour Party Conference. Time and again the effort has
been made to secure a decision there accepting the Communist Party itself as an affiliated party. The Labour Party
however has a keen nose for the scent of Moscow, and resists
resolutely such attempts to infiltrate its ranks. But 'eternal
vigilance' is called for, because the attempt is constantly
renewed, with pertinacity and cunning.

The Trades Union Congress is the assembly of all trade

1. Members may 'contract out' of this obligation.

unions, and it elects a General Council to act for it in discussions with the government and in other ways. Membership of this Council and of its Committees is of course open to Communists, if they can get themselves appointed. At the national level this is not easy. But locally the trade unions come together in Trades Councils. These have little executive power and limited importance in the trade union sphere proper. There is a tendency therefore to leave representation on Trades Councils either to the one or two real enthusiasts, or to less important people who are pleased to be distinguished in this way. Here again is an opportunity seized with both hands by the Communists, so that their predominance in some Trades Councils is even more marked than elsewhere in the trade union movement. In the Trades Councils they are often able to secure declarations of policy supporting the Communist Party line, declarations which are then publicised as being ostensibly those of the whole trade union movement in the area. This has happened repeatedly in London and in other cities of importance in Britain.

The membership of the Communist Party in this country has probably never been more than 100,000. It may now be between 30,000 and 40,000.[1] Most of its work is planned in complete secrecy, and much of it is carried through, as it were, in disguise. A favourite device is to sponsor, by the initiative of secret members, societies or movements attracting special groups, it may be of churchmen, actors, scientists, artists, teachers, pacifists, the unemployed, defenders of civil liberty, and so on. Many who have no real knowledge of the Party nor any intention of furthering its central purposes, have in this way been drawn into unwitting co-operation with it. Some have been brought under its influence and

1. Probably now substantially less following the Hungarian revolution of 1956, which exposed so clearly the power politics of the Soviet 'empire'.

used so constantly for its purposes that they have become 'fellow-travellers'. Experience in countries where Communism has become dominant shows clearly that the fellow-travellers are never allowed to develop any independence of thought or action. They are very soon either swallowed up in the Party, or 'liquidated' as 'unreliable elements', sometimes very brutally.

In Britain special attention is given by Communism to students and others from the colonial territories, or from similar countries outwith the Commonwealth. These young men will assume in their own countries in due course roles of leadership. If they can be indoctrinated, or recruited for the Party, if their grievances can be magnified and their sense of strangeness here exploited, they may become rebellious on their return. It is a great propaganda point for international communism if Britain is obliged to maintain good order in a colony by armed intervention. The strength of Britain is thus wasted, feeling is exacerbated against her among all dependent peoples, and even in this country some discontent may be caused among those who may have to serve in the armed forces in distasteful repressive campaigns.

The picture of Communism in Britain which emerges is something far different from that of a pitifully weak parliamentary political party. That particular role is quite unimportant in a Communist estimate in this country at the present time. As part of the international conspiracy of Communism we are faced here in Britain with something quite new in the world. There are here found together the ambition to rule and conquer, the discipline of an army, convinced belief in a harsh creed in which there is no place for the individual free personality of the human being, a quasi-religion in which impersonal historic inevitability of process takes the place of God. History has known the self seeking conqueror, the fanatic believer prepared to impose his will on all mankind, the completely committed servant of a cause, the conspirator working underground to achieve the sudden seizure of power, the adroit cynical politician making use of simple men and exploiting the generous sympathies of better men. Communism wherever it exists is all of these things, and because it is all of them, it transcends the limitations of each of them. It is a unique and immensely formidable organisation of belief and power, seeking more power to bring *all men* under its sway. It is in Britain, it is everywhere, and it is everywhere essentially the same.

If we are convinced by increasing knowledge of it that we must do whatever in us lies to oppose its expansion, questions arise to which we must seek clear answers, with the purpose of *acting* in accordance with these answers.

For the trade unionist the main question is, how can the Communist be curbed without witch-hunting McCarthyism, without damaging the freedom and vigour of the trade union tradition? Only the trade unionist himself can answer it, but he can answer it only in action, by actual presence and vigorous participation in meetings of the unions, at all levels, and in well thought out tactical combination with the genuine democrats among his fellow trade unionists. The main position of responsibility must be kept for men who will uphold the interests of the workers within the framework of our industrial system as a going concern, the improvement of which is to be sought by genuine democratic procedures.

The day to day representation of the workers in the factory is largely undertaken by shop stewards. These men stand at the points of friction in industry. Just because they are points of friction peaceable men are apt to avoid them, and leave them to the militants. The psychology of the situation favours the Communists. But these are also *key* points and no *key* points should be abandoned to those whose outlook justifies them in betrayal and subversion.

IX

The New Strategy of Communism

SINCE the death of Stalin early in 1953 there has unfolded by stages a change in Communism the inner nature and full extent of which it is difficult for even the best informed Western analysts to estimate. Internally it has been described as a 'thaw', externally, in the relations of the Soviet Union with other nations, as a 'relaxation of tension'. The leaders of Communism express a desire for 'peaceful coexistence', 'cultural exchanges', an increase in trade with the West, and a reduction in armaments all round.

In marked contrast with Stalin, the new leaders have travelled widely in promotion of these policies. They have reversed some of Stalin's most notorious practices, releasing large numbers of political prisoners, whether Soviet or foreign, bringing to an end by stages the huge slave labour camps, repudiating the right of the secret police to act outside the law, and restoring Tito to the fellowship of the Communist world with apologies for the mistakes made formerly by the Cominform in its treatment of the Yugoslav Communist Party and its leader. There are evidences of a more liberal attitude on the part of the government and Party to the ordinary Soviet citizen. Some degree of encouragement is now being given to personal travel, both of Soviet citizens abroad and of foreign tourists in the U.S.S.R.

Most remarkable of all the acts of the new régime was the deliberate denunciation by Khrushchev of Stalin's tyranny, in a long detailed speech at the 20th Congress of the Communist Party of the Soviet Union. *In large measure the critical verdict passed long ago by the West on Stalin's dictatorship, became at*

that Congress the official verdict of the Communists themselves.
The picture of Stalin's rule built up by Western students of
Communism was amply confirmed by the evidence of the
new First Secretary of the Party.

Does this mean that Communism has changed radically?
How far did the denunciation go?

Nothing in the main doctrine of Communism as originated
by Marx and developed by Lenin *and Stalin* has been dis-
carded. The Party, with its 'democratic centralism', remains
as Lenin shaped it. There are to be no other parties, nor,
within the Communist Party itself any organised dissent or
minority groups. 'Monolithic unity' is still required. What
has been expressly rejected is 'the cult of personality', by
which is meant the concentration of power in one supreme
leader, leading to the exaction by him of abject obedience
and extravagant adulation from all others. 'Collective
leadership' is now established, which seems to mean not only
that there is now a group of men sharing supreme authority,
but also that they recognise themselves to be no more than
man-size, and that they do not aspire to dictate personally,
as Stalin did, the 'correct' theories in science, the 'correct'
styles in architecture, music, literature and art. In contrast
to the morose, sardonic, coarse and suspicious traits that pre-
dominated in the personality of Stalin the new leadership
seems to cultivate a certain urbanity and candour in dealing
with other men.

But there is little evidence that the new leadership is
any more controlled by a public opinion freely formed
and freely expressed. Nor is it yet admitted that the tyranny
of Stalin was made possible by the absence in Russia of free
democratic institutions. A most un-Marxian explanation is
offered when Stalin's tyranny is attributed to personal defect
in him, amounting latterly to something like madness. In
earlier chapters we laid stress on Stalinism as a natural

[73]

development of the central principles of Communism itself. In support of this can be quoted the nature of Communism all over the world, seeing enemies everywhere, everywhere resorting to violence and lying accusations; obsessed with abstract theory, careless of the individual human being. World Communism has been singularly apt in learning from the monster who became its master. Since everywhere it has obediently echoed the new voices of the Kremlin, it is not yet certain how far Stalin has been genuinely repudiated. There is great difficulty in believing that a tyranny exercised for twenty years *through the Communist Party*, reveals nothing defective in the Party itself. It would seem that either it must remain at heart Stalinist, or must go much farther than Khrushchev in rejecting its past. There are encouraging signs that in some national communist parties this may happen. Some at least, in Poland, seem to wish to give more honest consideration to the needs and wishes of the working people. And elsewhere too there are signs that Tito's independence of Moscow is coveted. Whatever the non-communist can do to encourage these developments should be done, and we should be willing without compromising our own principles, to make the most of any opportunities for contact that may be offered, so that the unwholesome isolation in which the Communist countries have been held may be broken down.

Whatever the interpretation given by the Communists may be, there seems to have followed upon Stalin's death a mighty revulsion of feeling against the grey, harsh brutality of his régime. How far this feeling may carry Communism only the future will show. Conceivably it might carry it to a more searching re-examination of the political principles and the moral basis of the Marxist creed.

Meantime another factor has profoundly affected the relations of the communist and Western democratic worlds.

That is, the possession by both of the enormously expensive and immensely destructive hydrogen bomb. This has produced a situation in which neither side can risk a world war, and both must shape their policy to avoid it. Again, the history of Communism especially in Russia is of hope long deferred that maketh the heart sick. The repeated sacrifices of the people to build up heavy industry, to match the economic development 'of the most advanced capitalist nations' has never yielded its fruits in a high standard of living actually enjoyed. Partly this has been because of the expense of armaments. The influence of Communism in the world could no doubt be greatly extended if it were possible for the Soviet Union to devote part of its power to produce capital goods (the equipment of factories, power stations, agricultural tractors, railways) for exportation to the backward countries, such as India, Indonesia, Burma, Egypt, as well as China.

It is to be remembered too that, in the theory of Marxism-Leninism, the so-called capitalist countries require, for the stability and expansion of their economy, to find markets for their products by maintaining big armaments budgets. The conclusion from all these considerations may very well be that a new strategy is called for. By a conciliatory diplomacy the need for arms can be reduced and a big reduction in the military budgets of the West forced upon them. At the same time Russia will be enabled to send capital equipment abroad, cutting out Western competitors in these markets, and in due time enabling the economically backward countries to produce more of the goods required by their own people. The total effect might be such as to require big adjustments in the economic system of Britain and America and their allies. It is of course the conviction of the Communists that the 'capitalist' system is incapable of making such adjustments, being unplanned. The 'contradictions' within capital-

[75]

F

ism would become more marked in the conditions of a slump, as in the early 1930's and the prestige of the planned system of Communism would soar, and the task of propaganda become much easier.

If this is the new challenge of Communism, how is it to be met? Up till now the challenge has in a sense been easy to meet, because it has been the crude challenge of military power and political terror. Economically the Communist system has (except in the depths of the slump) seemed to be markedly inferior, and morally it has, under Stalin, been repulsive. But given the new strategy outlined above, the problem is greatly changed, and we must now devote some thought to its analysis.

X

The Task before the Democratic World

IN the first few weeks of the Korean War (1950–53) the
American General William F. Dean was captured, and spent
the next three years as a prisoner of the communist North
Koreans. He was not in a prisoner of war camp, and although
subjected to long hostile interrogations under conditions of
horrible discomfort when he was very weak and ill, and once
or twice threatened with torture he was never tortured in
the strict sense. The hardships he suffered through cold,
insufficient food, close confinement, and mental and moral
isolation were severe, and would have broken most men,
and certainly embittered them. But he survived without
bitterness, and is able from his experience of the world of
communism at close quarters to give a considered verdict
upon it, in certain aspects.

General Dean acknowledges that the physical conditions
of his life were not so very different from those of his guards.
At the end of his book[1] he says, 'the most important discovery
to me was that the ordinary communists who guarded me
and lived with me really believed that they were following
a route toward a better life for them and their children'. A
great part of the world is at least half convinced that this is
true, and that the Western democratic world stands in the
way and blocks their progress to that better life. How are
we to convince them that they are at least part wrong, that
ours is a better way and that they can share it, and we can go
on together without hatred and violence?

General Dean himself has some suggestions to make. 'We

1. *General Dean's Story*, Weidenfeld and Nicolson, 1954, p. 234.

[77]

must' he tells us 'present a better world than the communists. We must have an answer simple enough for the dullest to understand. We must each of us, really know the things for which we fight.'[1] Filling out this answer, he stresses three things: (1) our institutions, ensuring personal freedom and the right of every citizen to play his part without fear in the election of his government, (2) a high standard of living[2] and (3) a good standard of personal conduct. 'Every individual (he is speaking of an army) must realise that his whole country is judged by his *behaviour* . . . and not by the ideals to which he gives lip service.'[3]

It is generally recognised that for the millions of the world's poor men, the appeal of sufficient food, clothing, homes is direct and strong. But what appeals strongly to them is that they should get these things for themselves by getting to know the technique, by possessing the machines, by organising the job themselves. To know that in the West we enjoy a high standard of living is not convincing if they have any ground for suspecting that it is at their expense, by exploiting weaker peoples. Neither demonstrably superior technology and an immeasurably higher standard of life, nor fine words about freedom will convince unless by our behaviour, individually and communally we show ourselves willing to share these good things completely with them, helping them to possess them as their own in a relationship of

1. Op. cit., p. 235.   2. p. 235.
3. p. 134. 'If I were to try to change the mind of this convinced communist and could bring him to the U.S.A. to accomplish it I'm not sure that I'd bother to show him government buildings or legislatures at work, or even courts in which the accused has a chance for justice. Rather I'd take De Soon Yur to an American supermarket and walk him past a hundred foot meat counter. I'd like him to see in one minute more meat than he has seen in his entire life. . . . I'd like him to see the milking machines in a modern dairy, Kansas wheat elevators and an Iowa cornfield, a big knitting mill and a thousand sheep in a band.'

equality with us. Throughout the forty years of its history in Russia, Communism has made little progress in the actual standard of living enjoyed by her people. What has counted in holding the loyalty of the people, hard pressed, ill clad, often hungry, has been the feeling that Communism is *committed* to an acceptable social ideal, and has taken the first essential step to its achievement by doing away with the private exploitation of capital. So long as men are persuaded that the main things are sound, they will stand much incidental blundering and hardships in social life.

It is not just a pious platitude that man does not live by bread alone. It may be much more satisfying to the working men of any country to feel themselves secure and respected than to have an increasing pay packet. It may be much more important to a colonial people to feel themselves accepted in a genuine partnership with their former rulers than to make rapid industrial progress as clients of a powerful but patronising imperialism. The Central African Federation was formed with the purpose of providing greater opportunities for economic growth to the peoples of Southern and Northern Rhodesia and Nyasaland. But the significance of this increasing prosperity for the African will depend entirely on whether his social status, his dignity as a man, keeps pace with his improved material standards, or whether he suffers the moral degradation involved in white supremacy.

Philip Deane, English journalist captured in 1950 in Korea by the Communist forces, describes a conversation with a Korean intellectual who had been educated in the West. He freely acknowledged the superiority of the technology, of the culture, even of the political theories of Western democracy. But he felt that he and his people were excluded from full participation in this heritage. And he confessed himself a willing fellow-traveller with the Communists because they invite and urge the backward nations to full participation. Among them he was not a yellow man, race was of no account, and for him that was decisive.

The importance of this moral factor in human happiness cannot be too much stressed. Those concerned with children 'deprived of a normal home life' who are taken into the care of a Children's committee are fairly well agreed that to prevent them being unhappy and even delinquent is not easy. The Children's Officer may ensure that they have good food and clothing, nice toys, a well managed home. But unless the child has the security of spontaneous affection surrounding it, the restlessness remains. It is frequently found that a child is happier with his own parents even when they are rough, inefficient and dirty, because they are able to give him an entirely natural affection—not a wise affection, nor a sensitive affection, but, such as it is, genuine and unforced. On a higher level, a big tousy family, where things have often to be done without, but where everybody shares the joys and the hardships, and there are no favourites, is likely to be a much happier environment than, let us say, the millionaire's home with servants galore to wait upon a pampered only son.

It is from this point that we must take our bearings in the world as it now stands, with two great systems of belief and power facing each other in tension and competition, and the vast remainder of humanity in various stages of development and decision. Both the great systems are, of course, within themselves, far from homogeneous, unified, or static. Each could develop from its present condition towards irrational tyranny or towards more humanity and reason. We recall Hitler and Mussolini in the recent past of the West, we see McCarthy in America and Apartheid in South Africa, all of them portents in one case; and the present ambiguities of communist policy in the post-Stalin era are significant in the other.

From the inside, the civilisation of the West comprises as its main elements:

(1) *Science*, based upon free inquiry, and fostered by free publication; this involves a basic faith in the possibility of a rational knowledge of the natural world, and also of an impartial, objective study of society and its problems:

(2) Related to science is *technology* and invention, the application of science to the mastery of nature for human purposes; with this goes a belief in the importance for human wellbeing of controlling external circumstances[1]:

(3) Impressive progress made in the West in this sphere by the creation of modern manufacturing industry, commerce and communications, was begun and has for the most part been continued until now, by the system of free enterprise based on private property known as *capitalism*; part of this development has involved the organisation under Western leadership of the manpower and resources of countries possessed of limited technical knowledge and a feeble apparatus of production; in its fully developed form, involving political control, this has produced *imperialism* as a characteristic feature of the West:

(4) Alongside these achievements, Western civilisation has, partly under the influence of Christianity, partly under the influence of a rational humanism, accepted in theory, and applied substantially in practice, certain *moral ideas*; central among these has been a high valuation of free human personality, of the individual human being capable of rational thought and moral judgment, making his own choices; the recognition of fundamental rights of the individual by society has profoundly affected life in the West,

---

1. By way of contrast the Ancient World and Hindu civilisation believed more seriously in control of the mind, detaching itself from external circumstance and achieving a noble independence and sovereignty over circumstance.

and it is the sum total of these rights that we mean by democracy; they include the right of fair trial by an impartial tribunal, the right to take part without intimidation in the election of a government, the right to form one's own opinion on any matter and to express it by speech or printing, the right therefore to an education suitable to needs, the right to associate freely in the pursuit of any purpose not infringing the reasonable needs of others, the right to work under suitable conditions, or to maintenance on a modest standard at the charge of the community.

With these rights go the corresponding duties.

This is not of course an exhaustive account, even in outline, of the characteristics of our Western civilisation. It includes no reference to the arts, in which the West can claim great and distinctive achievement. Between these elements there is no complete harmony. For example, the scientific interpretation of man is not always easily reconciled with that which is derived from the Christian religion, yet both are powerful ingredients in our civilisation. Likewise, the relationships between men imposed by capitalist forms of economic organisation are not easily reconciled with democratic ideas of human relationship. The tension between capitalism and democracy has been a dynamic feature of Western civilisation for more than three hundred years, and its development has reached different stages and forms in different countries. In none of these countries has capitalism ever dominated the social scene. Democracy, or earlier, the Christian view of man from which democracy arises, have profoundly modified the impact of capitalism. To characterise our civilisation at any stage simply as capitalistic, is an absurd simplification and perversion. Yet it must be acknowledged that modern industrialism began very badly as a system of human relationships. From the point of view of its victims, the wretched slum-dwelling factory workers and miners of past generations, the exploited peoples of the colonies from the days of slavery to the colour bar of this century—to such people it had the feel not of an achievement enhancing human dignity but of an outrage against it. Even in Britain where democracy and capitalism together have brought into being the Welfare State, the evil past still bedevils industrial relations. How much more does the civilisation of the West tend to be marked in the eyes of 'colonial' peoples, by its history as they know it, by the character of domination, exaggerated by differences of colour between the ruling and the subject races.

What is of special importance in the tension and competition between the great systems of belief and power in the next generation, is that in the West the moral ideals which are at its heart, should penetrate more fully and convincingly its political and economic organisation. Only then will its technology become wholly attractive and be seen as a gift and not as a threat. Alliances which now are partly imposed on Eastern, Middle Eastern or African countries because of their dependence on our superior wealth and strength, will then be welcomed as partnerships to which all can give their committed allegiance. Even within the Iron Curtain the pull of a better civilisation will be felt, and Communism, in spite of false doctrine, will be impelled to develop its more humane elements.

Unless the moral fabric of the democratic West, internally as well as in its relations with other peoples, is made more sound, not as theory only, but in commitment and in practice, we shall be able to oppose to Communism, with all our material wealth and power, nothing but confusion, divided loyalty and groping indecision. This was our plight in Britain for seven unhappy years in face of the growing power of Hitler's Germany before the war—a power based on the tawdry philosophy of National Socialism. Communism is a sturdier and more respect-worthy creed than nazism. It is moral strength, in our institutions, our laws, our established social relationships and our personal thought and action, that we need to meet its challenge.

XI

The Importance of Institutions

So far we have been concerned mainly with communism, trying to achieve a clear and conscientious critical estimate of it as a theory and as a historic revolutionary force challenging our own life in the most serious way. Our critical estimate has been based on the democratic and Christian tradition in which we have grown up. It has been assumed that between Christianity and democracy there is a close affinity. The association between the two in our minds is almost instinctive. It is rooted in the conviction that before God all men are equal, equally His creation, equally under His judgment, equally the objects of His love. When Thomas Rainborowe in the debates of Cromwell's Army said that 'the poorest he that is in England hath a right to live as the greatest he', he was drawing from this religious conviction the conclusion that in the commonwealth everyone should count as a man, without diminution of the rights essential to his manhood. He and his colleagues were willing to express this conclusion in terms of a very radical form of democracy, both in Church and State. It involved the abolition of the special privileges and powers attaching to rank and wealth and high ecclesiastical office, and the institution of a republican and equalitarian society. Short of these extremes, it has since those times been increasingly believed in Protestant countries that the proper expression in political terms of the Christian view of man is some form of democracy.

Christianity Transcends Institutions. We must beware of too simple an identification of Christianity with democracy or indeed with any particular social institution. Christian faith and life are, in an important sense, independent of all institutions. A verse of a children's hymn of a past generation comes to mind:

> God hath given each his station,
> Some have riches and high place,
> Some have lowly homes and labour,
> *All may have His precious grace.*

The first three lines are naïve and too complacent. It is not an admissible claim that the wealth of the rich and powerful, and the poverty and suffering of the humble are quite simply the will of God. Indeed the opposite could be said with at least equal force—that the rich possess their wealth and oppress the poor in defiance of God's will. But it is true, and of supreme importance, to affirm that *all* may have God's precious grace. In slum or palace, to the well-born and talented, to the unwanted child of vicious parents, the grace of God is offered, and to each it is of supreme importance for his life. God's relationship to men, as Creator, Judge, Redeemer, transcends the limitations of particular situations, and so also the deepest relationships of men to each other transcend the limitations of those social institutions by which men are related as rich and poor, master and servant, sovereign and subject, etc. In Christ there is neither Greek nor barbarian, male nor female, bond nor free: all are one in Christ.[1] 'The Colonel's lady and Mrs O'Grady are sisters under the skin.'

So the Christian Church was born and was able to grow, in a society in many respects quite alien to it. For example, a prevailing feature of the Roman Empire was the institution of slavery—so widely prevailing and characteristic that St. Paul found it natural to refer to the division between slave and free as one of the great comprehensive divisions of man-

1. Paraphrasing Galatians, ch. 3, v. 28, and Colossians, ch. 3, v. 11.

kind, like male and female. Not only St. Paul, but the Christian Church as a whole, felt able to transcend this fixed legal relationship and transform it from within, as it were, rather than denounce it as inherently un-Christian. The Christian slave or owner of slaves was not thought to be at once a contradiction in terms; slaves and owners of slaves could be fellow Christians. The Christian owner would, of course, treat his slaves with consideration and care for their well-being, and the Christian slave would obey such an owner with special respect and understanding. In the long run this might lead to the actual freeing of the slave by due legal process, but this was not demanded as inevitable. Similarly the existing autocracy of the Roman Empire was accepted as an institution, without questioning its validity. It was even affirmed to be 'ordained of God', and Christians were told to 'honour the King'. Democracy hardly suggested itself as a possibility. The general attitude of the Church seems to have been something like this. All men, in the providence of God, have their established places in society. Their salvation—their most important interest as moral and spiritual beings—transcends the limitations imposed upon them by these established social relations. The gospel is equally relevant to all. If men accept the service of Christ, all their relationships will be profoundly affected—but by way of inspiring in them new attitudes and new ways of acting according to Christ's supreme commandment of love. There was no critical appraisal of the institutions themselves, no attempt at social revolution or even social reform.[1]

This general attitude has remained characteristic of the Church throughout its history, in ancient, medieval and

1. We have observed in chapter 1 that the 'communism' of the early Church in Jerusalem cannot be regarded as an attempt at social revolution. It assumed not the continuance of the Empire on a reformed basis, but its early supersession by a quite different kingdom of Christ.

modern times, in both Catholic and Reformed Communions. Current institutions are accepted; what is regarded as all-important is the faith and virtue of individual men. Where the exercise of social power is concerned, whether the power is socially conferred by birth or rank or office or wealth, the influence of the Church has been exerted to persuade or enjoin the actual possessors of power to look upon it as a gift of God to be used in a Christian way. Indeed from St. Columba to Frank Buchman a characteristic strategy of the Church has been to seek the conversion of influential men, accepting the social order that has given them their positions of influence.

Every System needs good men. Properly understood, this view of the relation between men and the institutions they live under, may be recognised as valid. A king, a judge, a cabinet minister, an industrialist, a trade union leader, a tribal chief, a newspaper proprietor, the father of a family, may be personally upright or crooked. It matters supremely that they should be the former rather than the latter. The conversion of a tribal chief (to take one example), may have the effect of leading a whole tribe from superstition and unclean heathenism to a wholesome simple Christian faith and life, without any fundamental change in the forms of tribal rule. Moreover, any system of social order requires to be morally vitalised by the personal integrity and vision of those who live in it. The father training his son in virtue, the steadfast judge resisting bribery and intimidation, the trader honest in his exchanges—men like these are the salt preserving society from corruption. No institutions can work well or last long without such men: any system is liable to break down through a failure of character in those who operate it. No system by itself ensures that those to whom it gives power will be wise and just and energetic. No system is proof against the evil effects of cruelty, sensuality, laziness, avarice in those to whom it entrusts power. Where there is no vision, under any system, the people perish.

There is plainly much truth in the view that moral inspiration is more important than organisation in creating and in maintaining a good society, and in particular that the social task of the Christian church is *to produce good men*, to serve at all levels and in all callings, whatever the social system may be.

It is perhaps inevitable that with this view there should be associated a tendency to conservatism in regard to institutions—the forms of social order. If what really matters is the virtue of men, and if *any* forms, more or less, can be used well or ill according to the good or bad wills of men, then there is no strong reason to change the forms of social order, and every reason to concentrate on influencing the men themselves, in their inward hearts and minds, and also in their outward actions.

Examples of the Importance of Institutions. Nevertheless, further reflection should convince us that the Church cannot always confine its interest to personal virtue, but must concern itself also with the criticism and reform of institutions.

(a) *Monogamous Marriage.* In at least one important part of social life the Church has never been in any doubt about the importance of institutions. In the matter of sexual life *it has insisted upon monogamous marriage as the only acceptable form of recognised relationship.* The rigorous imposition of monogamy does not by itself secure success and soundness in marriage and in family life. It may be true, also, that polygamy, or even polyandry, can be happy and healthy forms of marriage, and concubinage is a familiar and approved institution in the Old Testament. But experience has taught[1]

---

1. The Church has of course based its teaching about marriage upon the authority of the New Testament, but it has also seen that teaching to be justified by experience, and taught so.

that the most favourable conditions for achieving the mutual trust of husband and wife, and their single-minded co-operation in the care of children, are provided by the institution of monogamy—a special form of relationship between the sexes defined and protected by custom and law.

(b) *Slavery*. We have already considered slavery as an example of an institution transcended and transformed by Christian faith and love. We may now take it to illustrate the seriousness of a bad institution. The essence of slavery is that one man is treated as the property of another. He is subject to his owner's will. He cannot in any complete sense exercise the essential freedom of a man to decide his own actions. The slave is reduced to thinghood, or at best to the status of a superior kind of domestic animal. The attempts made to justify the institution in fact always take the form of asserting, or seeking to show, that the slave belongs to a class or kind inherently deficient in certain of the essential properties of humanity, such as the capacity for rational thought. So far as a Christian slave owner may have chosen to treat his slaves as men and brothers he was really substituting another relationship for that of master and slave, something like that of an elder to a younger person. Both in ancient times and in nineteenth-century America, nominal legal slavery often assumed a milder character and real mutual respect between unequals was achieved. But strictly, legal slavery, giving complete control to one man, and requiring complete obedience from the other, is incompatible with any fully satisfactory human relationship. It tends to produce irresponsibility on both sides, cruelty in the master, shiftiness and deceit in the slave. Its existence in any society makes for the moral debasement of its members. In the end the only morally satisfactory way to deal with this institution is to abolish it.

(c) *The State and War*. In politics, the importance of

institutions can be simply and powerfully illustrated from the history of England and Scotland. For many centuries while these were independent kingdoms they were frequently at war, always suspicious and uneasy even in peace. In 1707 the Treaty of Union brought them under one government and they have never fought each other since.[1] This beneficent change was brought about by a new institution, a single parliament, an undivided government ruling both countries as the *United* Kingdom of Great Britain. After 1707 the peoples of Scotland and England were neither more nor less *virtuous* than before. They were simply living under different social arrangements—under *one* political sovereignty instead of *two*.

Such a union of sovereignties has not taken place, as yet, in any form, between the nation-states of Western Europe. The immeasurable effect of this circumstance on millions of men in this century is painfully clear. Wars between them have been frequent. Vast amounts of wealth and huge exertions have been directed to mutual destruction. It can be confidently affirmed that the people of America have been saved a similar experience[2] by the fact of federation in one sovereignty as the United States. Had the development of the great rich territories of the continental area of North America been carried out under the independent sovereignties of the original states, rivalries would have led to wars, and the interior condition and the external influence of

1. The rebellion of 1745 based on Scottish soil was a civil war both in Scotland and England. Whether the Treaty of Union was in every respect *the best way* of unifying the government is not here relevant.
2. Federation of course may be said to have involved the United States in a destructive *Civil War* over the question of slavery. But it was nevertheless a great gain for America that *only* this war, bitter and costly as it was, has taken place between the States which united to declare their Independence in 1776 and later cemented that union in a permanent federal constitution.

America would be far behind its present stage of progress.

In face of these considerations it is quite insufficient for the Church to attribute war simply and comprehensively to sin or moral defect in men, and to look for the abolition of war to the conversion of men's wills to righteousness. War is itself an institution, arising out of other institutions. What is required for its abolition is the fashioning of new forms of political sovereignty.

(*d*) *Stalinism*. For another illustration we may look once more at the case of Stalin. It has been shown that in re-nouncing Stalinism in its extremer forms, Khrushchev attri-buted its evil to the personal character of Stalin, and drew no adverse conclusions regarding the institutions which had permitted him to acquire excessive power and to exercise it in evil ways. Khrushchev did not recognise that in a par-liamentary democracy, it is exceedingly difficult for one man to achieve unchallenged authority, while on the other hand the single party dictatorship, and the institutions of 'demo-cratic centralism' encourage the concentration of power, and make a Stalin all too easily possible.

These examples demonstrate that, as a factor quite distinct from the moral *dispositions* of men, institutions have immense importance in forming the moral *relationships* of men in society.

There is a reciprocal influence between men and institu-tions. Good men can indeed make even bad institutions tolerable, and bad men can make good institutions hurtful. But good institutions can assist goodness in men and hinder evil. Bad institutions encourage evil and impede goodness. It is surely important that the Christian should concern him-self not only to make powerful men good, but also to co-operate in devising institutions that confer power upon good men. To speak less absolutely, since all men are mixed some-what of good and evil, it is a Christian concern to ensure that the basic relationships of men, defined by the institutions of society, are such as to encourage their goodness and restrain their evil.

The discussion so far has referred mainly to the primary Christian interest in moral goodness in men. But Christianity has an interest also in human happiness as that depends on material well-being. Much activity is necessarily devoted by men to the improvement of their own lot by procuring the means of life for themselves and their dependents. There is a natural and inevitable 'selfishness' in men, inherent in the will-to-live. This can lead to strife and exploitation, but it can be guided to co-operation. A good exchange in the market-place, for example, satisfies the self-regarding interests of both parties. It involves what might be called 'selfish co-operation' between them. Many social institutions are devised to faciliate such selfish co-operation. The Christian has an obligation to assist in this work of social order for the sake of ordinary human happiness.

Occasions arise in the course of human history when old institutions prove inadequate for the purposes of human virtue or happiness. Let us take by way of illustration the famous Tennessee Valley Authority of the United States of America. Modern technology made possible in the huge area of the Tennessee Valley a number of related enterprises, including the control of flood water, the prevention of erosion of the soil, afforestation, the generation of electrical power, the development of industries requiring that power, the provision of cheap fertilisers for agriculture, the improvement of agricultural methods through education and mechanisation, the improvement of navigation. These schemes were all dependent on the building of a series of dams on the river Tennessee and other works involving the property of many hundreds of private persons and corporations. In order that these many interdependent enterprises (amounting together to a revolutionary transformation in the ways of life and standards of living of a great part of the population of the whole valley) might be carried out, it was necessary to devise a new type of institution (TVA) with powers to compel the necessary co-operation of property owners in the area. Old views of the rights inherent in the ownership of property had to be substantially modified, if this massive improvement in the economic and social life of the valley were to be achieved.

The devising of institutions suitable to the needs and possibilities of human relationship is of the utmost importance for human well-being. An institution may be described as a technique or method defining relationships or behaviour so as to deal effectively with some permanent or recurring situation in human life. It may be established by custom and habit or by law. A good institution fixes responsibility; it imposes a code of conduct. It may promote active co-operation or merely prevent quarrelling ('good fences make good neighbours'). For some time the development of industry and commerce was held up because no satisfactory method had been found of organising the investment of capital by a large number of small investors in one enterprise. To the risk of losing his own investment was added the risk of having to accept responsibility for the debts of the whole company without limit. This encouraged the reckless investor, and discouraged the prudent. The invention of the limited liability joint stock company transformed the situation. It at once made readily available investment savings that would formerly have been hoarded, or applied only to 'safe' subjects such as land.

Institutions define or impose or at least express a structure of human relationship. Some are so well established and successful that they seem almost part of the nature of things. But about an institution there is always something artificial.

It is a social device related to particular needs and circumstances, and can, and should, be changed to suit changing circumstances.

The relationship of employer and employee for example is an invention of men. Even in its simplest and most 'natural' form it involves a bargain or contract of some kind. At its simplest it may involve hiring on the employer's terms and firing without notice at his pleasure, and come very near to the institution of slavery. Under present circumstances in socially advanced countries, it involves quite complicated features. Usually the employer must by virtue of agreement with a trade union pay certain minimum wages, and observe stated conditions regarding hours and holidays, working arrangements, etc. The dismissal of a worker is subject also to various conditions, and, while he is in employment, certain payments must be made by him and by the employer on his behalf for insurance against unemployment, sickness and accident. The basic relationship of employer-employee remains, but its detailed character is much changed by closer definition in relation to a variety of circumstances.

A very great part of the life of every one of us is controlled by the institutions of the society in which we live—institutions supported by custom or law. Our membership in a family, our place in an industry, our citizenship in a particular nation, define for us a great part of the total pattern of our lives. The importance of the institutional framework within which we live may not be fully appreciated so long as it works well. But, when institutions break down, we are forced to see their importance. So long as our economic system provided normally the opportunity for most men to earn a livelihood that they considered satisfactory, no one worried too much about it. But when millions found it impossible to obtain work, the economic system began to be seriously examined. So long as nations live in peace, the system of independent nation-states is happily accepted. But when millions of men are ranged against each other in wars between these states, and great resources are devoted in time of peace to maintain armed forces for the defence of each nation's independence, questions force themselves upon us concerning the usefulness of the nation-state as a form of social organisation.

We are living in a period when many of the traditional institutions that have formed the framework of our lives are being questioned. They seem no longer adequately to achieve their purposes. Instead of promoting co-operation between men they seem often to force us into strife or confusion. It becomes very important that we should devise new institutions, new basic relationships, supported by custom and law, upon which we can count as settled things, to give us security for the planning of our individual lives.

XII

Power and Its Distribution

Is man a Rational Being? In thinking about themselves men are constantly inclined to fall into error by substituting abstractions for reality. For example, it is clear that the capacity for rational thought is one mark of humanity. It is however a mistake to go on from this fact to a general conception of man as rational, if we forget that man is also rooted in the natural order; that he is a special kind of animal, a creature of instinct, of habit, dependent on his senses, influenced by emotions, born an ignorant infant and growing up slowly, developing his full powers under the influence of custom, and the power of his parents and others. When all this is taken into account, his rationality is seen in a new perspective, and may amount (in certain situations) to little more than what the psychologists call rationalisation—a need to give himself and other people reasons for doing what his irrational habits and instincts suggest. *Just how reason works in man, actual man, is a question not answered by describing man in the abstract as rational.*

Liberal Democracy. The tendency to impose upon real life the abstractions of theory has been displayed habitually in political judgment. Liberal democracy arose in part from the rationalistic 'enlightenment' of the eighteenth century and the French and American revolutions of that period. It tended to exaggerate the rationality of man, and to represent the state as a voluntary partnership of its members co-operating in the enlightened pursuit each of his own interests. It was on the basis of this view that the expansion of democracy largely took place. Since men, it was argued, are

rational, they have a capacity and a natural right to participate in government. Education will rectify any defects of
actual knowledge they may have, and government by discussion and majority decision will be carried on, peacefully
yielding the greatest happiness to the greatest number. The
economic system of capitalism was represented as a system in
which such free rational co-operation was at its maximum.
Every man was 'economic man', an enlightened calculator
of values, buying in the cheapest and selling in the dearest
market, prudently comparing future advantage with present
need. It was for a time widely and sincerely believed that the
steady application of this assumption to the making of policy
would yield the maximum advantage to the maximum
number of people. The last grand expression of this theory
was in the League of Nations. It was thought that by giving
each natural grouping of men (each nationality) political
sovereignty, and by bringing their representatives, freely
elected, together to discuss their relations with one another
openly, peaceful agreed solutions to all problems would
normally be found.

Protestant Christiantiy tended to identify itself with some
such view of democracy and capitalism. It combined with this
a tendency to think of man as *essentially spiritual,* and *essentially individual*, each man being capable of independent decision, whatever the circumstances of his life, material or social.

The positive side of all this theorising about man must not
be underestimated. A rational morally responsible soul is
discerned in every man. Such a man is worth educating, he
may be entrusted with the vote, given leave to form associ-
ations. Among such men free publication, free inquiry, may
safely proceed. 'Great is truth and will prevail.' Modern
social progress, the impressive achievements of modern science and technology are largely the product of this liberal
rational view of man.

Another View of Democracy. Liberal democracy fails seriously to take account of the real nature and situation of men. *It is possible to give a justification of democracy based on an almost opposite and not less realistic appreciation of the facts of human life.*

As an example, take the *freedom of publication.* Far from being trustworthy in the use of this freedom, men will, if they have the power, use the press to promote opinions and foster prejudices favourable to their own interests. They will distort facts, they will suppress unwelcome truths, they will interpret complex situations to their own advantage. This may be done wittingly or under the pressure of unconscious impulses.

Sometimes it is suggested that some kind of censorship should be established. It should be entrusted to reliable men to decide what is worthy of publication. This is done in a special way by the Roman Catholic Church, which examines books to see whether they are worthy of the 'imprimatur' or approval of the Church. In the Soviet Union a much more rigorous system refuses the right of publication altogether to books or newspapers or magazines that do not accept the Marxist philosophy. But who is to ensure that the censor's power is not abused? The democratic answer is to allow a general freedom of publication within wide limits, so that every point of view may find expression. Errors and deceptions may then be criticised and exposed, and out of the competition of views, the truth may have a reasonable possibility of emerging.

Consider also *the democratic method of majority decision.* Among rational men, after free discussion, unanimity ought to be possible and a majority is likely to be right—such is the liberal principle. The realist principle might be stated in this way. Among men varying in interest, circumstance, ability and outlook no unanimity is to be expected even after prolonged discussion. But the practical needs of life require decision—the Queen's government must be carried on. A majority vote may be right or wrong, wise or foolish, but it is the one actually supported by most and therefore likely to be carried out and made effective. The minority, because it is a minority, will be inclined to accept it, and something will be done. Majority decision is a reasonably good practical device of government, and not much more.

Again, consider the history of the extension of the franchise to the point at which all adults, male and female, are given the vote. Against the liberal theory it may be affirmed that the vote was in fact conceded only to growing power. It is when the demand for the vote is backed by power, when those denied the vote are able to make a nuisance of themselves, that the possessors of state authority admit the newcomers to share their power. The appeal to justice is not answered until those who make it are able to demand justice because they have organised their strength.

The State as an Organ of Power. The relations of men to each other are relations of power. The state is *par excellence* the social organ of power. What distinguishes a government from other organs of social life is the extent of its power over all who come under its authority. This is often symbolised by the use of some emblem such as the lion or the eagle, each irresistible in its own domain. Other societies exercise power over their own membership. But membership in them is voluntary, or partly so. The ultimate sanction available to non-government organs is exclusion from membership (excommunication from the Church, expulsion from the school or club), but government can compel people to be and to remain members of the state, and to perform the duties of citizenship by threatening them with deprivation of all that makes life worth living, or even of life itself. In a very complete way government is an expression of power, and politics is the answer to the questions, by whom, for what purpose, in what ways, is this power to be used. Political history is largely the story of the struggles of dynasties, factions and classes to possess themselves of this power, the struggle of organised groups already possessing some power (military or economic or psychological) to extend it so as to control the whole power of the state. What constitutes the power of the state is a complicated question. It is lodged in a number of institutions, the army and police, the law courts, the civil service and so on, the whole forming what may be called an engine of power. Those who control the levers that activate this engine are the *de facto* government. Political activity involves a struggle to gain control of these levers, or keep control of them.

Our democratic system tends to disguise this fact from innocent eyes. Democratic government is sometimes called government by discussion, and the contrast between it and dictatorship is sometimes made by speaking of decisions reached by *ballots* as opposed to those reached by *bullets*. Anyone who has taken part in an election must know that this contrast can easily be made too absolute. Superficially an election may seem to be decided by argument and persuasion only. But in fact much depends on a well organised party machine, access to newspapers with a big circulation, plenty of cars on the day of the poll, the psychological force of spell-binding oratory, and other expressions of mere power.

This element in the political struggle was more evident in the days when rival pretenders to a throne met in actual combat. It becomes obvious when organised masses demonstrate in the streets of the capital city and armed revolutionaries seize the telephone exchange, power stations, the arsenal, parliament bulidings, and so on.

A phrase like 'the party in power' must be taken literally.

It is in a position to make the laws and enforce them by police action, and, if necessary, to break the power of any opposing organisation. A new government arising in a disordered country is usually 'recognised' by other states when it is seen to be unmistakably wielding the actual powers of a government. The former *de jure* government ceases to be recognised when it is seen to be no longer able to exercise coercive power within its own territory.

I emphasise this somewhat insistently because Christians in democratic countries often fail to recognise this essential feature of all government, and fail therefore to understand politics. While they are earnestly discussing the merits of a policy their more realistic opponents may be seizing control of the engine of power—and then all discussion ceases. Coming up against this feature in political life, even in its less stark forms in a democracy, the Christian may feel disgusted and disillusioned, and may retreat quickly from politics as a 'dirty business'. Or he may confine his participation to the milder and less direct ways of exercising power, by voting for the parties that seem to be less contentious and aggressive, the conservative centre parties.

Political innocence may show itself in another way. The moralistic approach may expect too much from legislation, not realising that legislation must be made effective against elements in society which may have to be coerced by sheer state power. The earnest moralists of Prohibition learned this in America, when the power of the state proved insufficient to enforce the law (carried by a substantial majority of voters) against the determined disobedience of the minority.

By contrast with the Christian democrat the Marxist exaggerates the element of power in the state and in politics. The state is for him the means by which the strongest economic class completes its domination over the other classes. The laws, he believes, are framed and administered in the interests of that class. In his own communist state the law-making body and the law courts are firmly subordinated to the executive, or rather to the small central group which controls the dominant Communist Party. And in any communist country an extraordinary importance attaches to the secret police, the distinguishing feature of which is not so much its secrecy as the fact that it operates outside the law, according to the arbitrary will of the dictator or dictatorial group, as an instrument of naked ruthless power.

It follows from this that to some extent it is true to say that 'the only argument the communist understands is the argument of superior force', and also that the Christian and the democrat with their habitual underestimate of the place of power in politics are often the easy victims of the communist. This however is a simplification of the position. The communist knows well that government cannot rest simply on naked power. It must evoke the consent, and if possible the loyalty, of the governed in support of its power. But even in this connection communist governments have relied heavily on mere propaganda, often deceitful, to secure that loyalty and consent. This is really coercion again, by psychological means. Marxist thinking, and still more communist action, have done much to bring home to democrats and to Christians the importance of power in the ordering of social life.

It should be noticed that persons or groups secure in the possession of power are often unaware of the extent to which their authority rests upon that foundation. A dominant class thinks of itself as deserving its privileges, and as conferring benefits upon the classes dominated, by the energy and experienced wisdom of its rule. A millionaire with several mansions, a shooting lodge, luxury cars, a well appointed yacht, a racing stable, a private golf course, an aeroplane, and his wife with gorgeous clothes and jewellery, do not think of themselves as consumers of an inordinate amount of wealth. They think of themselves as patrons, giving remunerative employment to chauffeurs, gardeners, stable boys, tailors, and so on. They do not realise that only the power that wealth commands enables them to keep their wealth. Communism has exposed for us very clearly the element of sheer power in this sort of relationship.

Distribution of Power in a Democracy. Democracy is a system of government by which power is distributed over the whole adult population, and by which the needs and desires of the whole people are conveyed to representatives exercising direct power on their behalf. It is noteworthy that communism challenges the adequacy of our western parliamentary democracies on the ground that they are only nominally democratic. The relations of power within society, they say, are determined by the fundamental economic relations. Where property in the means of production is privately held and unequally divided, the power of the poorer classes is insufficient to enable them to exercise fully their political rights. The press, for example, is owned and directed by rich men, and is used to deceive the electors by its distorted presentation of the facts of social life. Men are thus induced to vote for policies that are harmful to their own interests. As the necessary condition for a true democracy (in the language of communism a 'people's democracy') they say that the economy must be socialist—the means of production must be owned by the whole people. In particular the newspapers and other organs of information must be controlled by responsible bodies like trade unions, the army, the Communist Party, answerable to the appropriate ministers in a 'people's government'.

In view of the actual state of the press in this and other democratic countries it is difficult to give a fully satisfactory answer to this kind of charge. The example of the B.B.C.

and the first attempts to establish a Press Council in Britain may suggest that there are possibilities still to be explored within the framework of our own democracy for the creation of a more socially responsible press, still possessing sufficient freedom to act as forceful critic of public policy.

But with all that may be said against our imperfect democracy it can be claimed that actual experience has shown that in it a working-class party can organise effectively, get itself elected into power, and use its power in legislation and administration. By contrast, in communist countries hitherto, governments have been unwilling to allow any opposition to organise itself, and even on the basis of a complete socialist economy have denied to the people the free exercise of their constitutional rights. *It is on the face of it in these countries that democratic institutions remain nominal. Real power instead of being widely distributed is notoriously concentrated in the hands of either one man or a small collective leadership.*

It has been mentioned that no government, even the most uninhibited tyranny, can depend wholly on naked power. It must rely largely on the consent and seek to evoke the positive loyalty of the people it rules. This is especially true in its relations with other states, but it is important also within its own domains. Unless it can count on the willing participation of individuals and groups in execution of its plans there will be neglect, confusion or obstruction in greater or less degree, and the plans will go awry.

To put the matter another way, government power, although more extensive than that of any other social organ, is limited, and depends upon the power of various sorts residing in other social groupings. Unless these groups are allowed to organise themselves in accordance with their own needs and standards, and to develop their own limited but real autonomy they cannot function well. For example, if scientists are not allowed to have their own periodicals, to control their own laboratories and promote their own programmes of research and teaching, and formulate and communicate the theories resulting from their experiment and observation, they just cannot be scientists. If industrial enterprises cannot try out new materials, new machines, new methods of organising production, and test them by their own criteria of efficiency and economy, they cannot play their proper part in the commonwealth. The same may be said about Churches, teaching their members and ordering their worship in accordance with their own apprehension of moral and spiritual reality. Successful government that really conserves and nourishes the life of the people, must respect the limits of State power, and recognise the proper spheres of other social organs in the community, right down to the family, in some respects the most fundamental social group of all. Totalitarian government, with its pretensions to direct all activity within the State, providing not only funds but inspiration, protecting the citizens not only from crime but from their own errant thoughts, is gravely weakened in the end, because it cannot generate the spontaneous healthy energies of its own constituent groups and citizens. Democratic life built up from the bottom by allowing every element in the community to make its own natural power felt, is more flexible, responsive to need, and in the long run stronger.

XIII

Christian Political Realism

In the first chapter of this book attention was drawn to a number of ideal visions of the good society which were characterised as Utopian. These were not directly concerned with the reformation of existing society. The question, *How* are they to be realised? was not seriously asked. The power of God was invoked, but how men might make themselves the instruments of that power was hardly considered. However legitimate this neglect of the question of power may be in the visionary, it cannot be evaded by the Christian in a democracy, where he is given a share in the power of the state, and must as a citizen take his part in deciding how that power is to be used. Many Christians have a conscientious difficulty about power, which is at its most acute in relation to the use of military power in war. It is sometimes thought that power is in itself, when used for the coercion of other men, a contradiction of love. It is suggested that if love were pure enough it would itself have power to transform opposition into co-operation.

This attitude, never consistently applied, but present as a scruple impeding full activity in the body politic, fails to take account of the real circumstances of human life.

God Himself in the belief of Christians is acknowledged as all powerful and this is not just another way of saying that He is all loving. Over all His creatures, wholly dependent upon Him but having an existence distinct from His, He has complete power—the power to make, the power to destroy, the power to uphold or to frustrate their purposes. It is assumed here that power and love are distinct, that God uses

His power in accordance with His purposes of love and that therefore power can be so used. Our own life is based on power over the lower creatures, and no order in society is possible without power. The authority of the parent over the child, of the teacher over the class, of the chairman over the meeting, of the employer over the employee, is or includes an element of power. Custom and law prescribe in all these cases limits within which power can be exercised. But within these limits the community affords the support of its power, ultimately of its police and military power, to the authorities concerned. In a well-ordered society direct power is seldom used, but in a well-ordered society it is always available when required. We may never personally knock a man down, or hold him back. But when we depend on other people to do this for us if necessary, *we are using force.* It is safe to say that whenever we use money or vote, or lock our doors, or pay our income tax, or send our children to school, or accept an appointment in competition with others we are using or submitting to force in some way that is quite necessary for civilised human life.

The Importance of Social Order. This becomes evident whenever for some reason social order breaks down—property is insecure, money becomes useless, plans cannot be made. In such a situation almost any power capable of imposing order will be welcomed. Before social groups can function, even simple social groups, 'someone has to be in charge'. So important is mere order that any government, even a tyranny or an incompetent government, represents a universal human interest. It is from this point of view that government as such, the State, must be regarded as an ordinance of God. So Martin Luther felt when he supported the constituted authority of the princes against the rebellious peasants. So any society must give some authority to its chairman and support his ruling, even when that ruling may not be altogether wise. The paramount need for order, if a recognisably human life is to be lived, is so great that any given order once established has amazing powers of endurance, and may last through centuries essentially unchanged, attaching to itself the support of morality and religion, and indicting all innovators as unnatural, inhuman and atheistic, and yielding to its supreme authority, a reverence bordering on worship, or actually becoming such.

Any given social order is a balance of powers and interests, an equilibrium of forces liable to be disturbed by innovations in any direction. To secure preservation of the balance there is a strong tendency in human societies to affirm of any actually existing equilibrium that it is part of the order of nature itself, unchangeable, the will of God. The hazards of life are great enough to incline men to keep to the tried and known ways. Politics from this point of view is the art of building up, maintaining and commending to men an ordered balance of interests and powers. The authority of government depends to a large extent on the discernment with which it recognises the actual strength of the various interests and proposes policies which reflect this balance, adapting itself to significant changes in the internal balance of social powers with a minimum of disturbance to the old forms of social order. It is in this respect that the British 'genius for government' has shown itself through most of the changes, religious and economic, that have developed during several centuries. The most notable example is the monarchy, still formally the supreme authority, but responsible through successive shifts of power to the landed aristocracy, the middle classes, the working classes or various combinations of them as each rose to influence in Parliament. Notable instances of failure were the seventeenth-century troubles concerning religion, and the secession of the American colonies. Hopeful experiments in the admission of new elements to power are going on now in the further evolution of the British Empire into a Commonwealth of equal nations. Broadly the justification of all conservative politics lies in this need for order in social relationships. The basic assumption of conservative politics is that whatever social order has successfully maintained itself has done so because it has *done justice* to existing social interests and forces and has existed, implicitly at least, with the consent of the governed. This is to say that order is related to justice, for people will not be consenting to the order of society unless they are accorded such rights as will enable them to lead the sort of life of which they feel themselves capable.

However, men's sense of their own capabilities changes. When for the first time laymen read the Bible in their own language and realised fully how different was New Testament teaching from the doctrine and practice of their priests, they began to feel capable of decision in matters of religion and to demand various sorts of reformed Church in some of which laymen would continue to play a more responsible part. When workers united first for mutual support in sickness and adversity they began by stages to realise that they might unite in defence of their interests (through trade unions) *vis à vis* their employers, and then to feel capable of voting for Parliament, and even of sitting in Parliament and entering cabinets, and finally, of forming governments.

Because of these changes, conservatism is not enough; the old order must either be adapted to accommodate new forces of social life or be transformed by gradual or revolutionary change to a new order. Maximum continuity of order with sufficient change is the ideal formula.

This conclusion sounds very comfortable. It implies that in the long run, taking a comprehensive view, both conservatives and reformers have their place in society, and it may suggest that some compromise between them is normally the right course. But it is a mistake to allow this view to degenerate into a hazy vagueness of judgment (or an un-committed attitude) in political questions. At any given moment decision is required and it may sometimes involve a sharp conflict, and what is felt to be a difficult reorganisation involving the risk of some degree of breakdown in social order. Recent instances in British experience are the decision to give independence to India in 1947 and the decision about the same time to provide a comprehensive national health service. No decision can be taken unless men are willing to commit themselves.

I am pleading here for Christian participation in politics. The whole argument of this book has been a plea for *Christian political realism* in relation to the changing social institutions of our time.

Christian political realism, involving participation in the contest for power and in the use of power, is by no means a formula that solves all problems. Indeed it raises many, and the answers are to be found for different people in different directions. Before we attempt to consider some concrete examples, it is necessary to take note of the kind of guidance offered to us by Christian teaching.

We may begin from the well-known aphorism of St. Augustine, 'Love God, and do what you like.' What this means is that, if a man love God with heart and soul and strength and mind, he has in that love alone a sufficient motive and guide for all his conduct. It is assumed that his *knowledge* of God is a Christian knowledge, that it is derived from God Himself through Christ and is a knowledge of God as the Father of our Lord Jesus Christ, a knowledge of the love of God as exemplified and interpreted in the life and teaching of Christ. *Do what you like*—this is at once a charter of Christian freedom and an unlimited demand. A Christian

will wish to do only what the love of God suggests or requires. In doing that he will feel himself free *from the limit-*
ations of the codes and special loyalties of his particular
community. This freedom is well illustrated in the instance
of the family. Jesus, broadly, says two things about the
family, one strongly positive, the other sharply negative. On
the positive side he affirms the supreme importance of the
family as the source of our very highest ethical experience by
his use of the words 'father' and 'son' to describe his own
relationship to God. This implies the cherishing of the
family as a school of love. On the negative side he demands
that the special obligations of family life should not be
allowed to prevent a man committing himself to the larger
discipleship of the 'Kingdom'. The family is not playing its
true part in the moral education of its members if it claims
an exclusive loyalty from them, and keeps them from giving
their love to all men. Christian love must feel itself free to
break the limiting bonds even of this special loyalty. But
this must be for the sake of love, to fulfil in other relationships with fellow-men the best lessons taught by membership
in the family. The freedom love demands is simply the
freedom to love, and this, of course, involves the willingness
to accept all the burden of love. The freedom that Jesus
claimed from the Sabbath law became in Gethsemane the
constraint that forced him to the Cross.

But when this is said, and with the utmost emphasis, to
assert the absolute character of the law of love as the supreme
and only law of Christian ethics, it should at the same time be
made plain that Christian teaching does not countenance an
abstract individualism, cutting a man off from the particular
situation in which the providence of God has placed him.

Forty years ago a boy of my acquaintance competed
successfully for a scholarship in a famous school. He was at
the time under strong religious influence and it seemed to

him that by taking his scholarship he was certainly depriving some other boy, maybe more needy, of a wonderful opportunity. He asked himself whether he should give up the scholarship. This may seem to common sense a foolish notion. It would have made nonsense of the whole system by which these scholarships were given, a system designed to choose the ablest pupils for the privileges of higher education, some degree of need having been first ascertained by confining the competition to those of limited means. Granted that in the then condition of educational provision it was a desirable thing that such scholarships should be open to the child of relatively poor parents, it would seem a perverse scruple to refuse a golden opportunity fairly won for the sake of satisfying an abstract Christian principle that it is better to give than to receive or that love demands sacrifice of our own happiness to the needs of others. In this particular situation, given the talents he had, given the scholarship system, given the slender resources of his parents, it was surely in accordance with love that he should accept the scholarship, but with a sense of privilege and responsibility, and a determination to make the best of his opportunity to equip himself for a fruitful career, as, in fact, the boy did, with great advantage to his fellow-men.

This is a typical situation for men. None of us has unlimited possibilities of fulfilling the law of love. A child is in immediate and special relations of obligation and dependence to his own parents, a citizen to his own town and nation. We all have a whole series of special relationships defining the possibilities of our lives. We owe a special duty to the group of which we are members, defined by the nature of our membership.

Much harm is done from a failure to recognise this limitation of our creaturely condition, the failure to recognise that we can never start from anywhere but *where we are*, and a consequent failure to do the utmost that love suggests within the limits of the possible.

Illustrations may be found in many fields. The fond parent may form ambitions for his child and set a target of attainment for him that is far beyond his capabilities. His love for his child may prove disastrous in forcing upon him an impossible task, producing either a sense of anxiety and guilt in his failure, or vigorous rebellion. The ecclesiastical perfectionist, forbidding divorce, may succeed only in maintaining unhappy unions, and even creating conditions favourable to adultery. Some of the dreadful energy of communist tyranny comes from the impatient desire to create a classless society now, very soon, without regard to human nature as it is, or existing institutions and habits. Not some improvement starting from where we are, but the immediate realisation of an ideal possibility, guides the actions of these perfectionists.

Other sorts of absolutism in ethics are sometimes found. Among religious people three forms may be distinguished.

(1) The perfection of God's will is seen to be not immediately practicable in the world, and this is taken to be a permanent situation. The world is regarded as a kingdom of darkness, under the rule of Evil, and hope is fixed upon Heaven as the realisation of God's Kingdom. Effort is then concentrated on winning men *from* the world for citizenship in Heaven. In the world men must keep themselves unspotted by confining themselves to the minimum participation in its life. This is typical of certain sects, marked by the 'narrowness' of their outlook. They tend to form a community within the community, and they mark off the division between themselves and 'the world' as sharply as possible. Love to fellow-men tends with such sects to be best shown by strenuous preaching, often invoking fear, as a means of persuading others to leave a doomed world and

join those who regard themselves as pilgrims on the way to Heaven, the only virtue of their sojourn on the earth being that it tests their faith.

(2) A special form of this absolutism is more characteristic of Roman Catholic Christianity. In Catholicism provision is made for withdrawal from the world by maintaining special communities, visibly detached from the normal life of the citizen and devoted in monasteries to the concentrated practice of the 'religious' life, by prayer and meditation, or by a vocation to 'good works' primarily undertaken as an exercise in virtue or as a mortification of their own souls. The vows of the members of such communities are those of poverty, chastity and obedience, the renunciation so far as may be of the natural life and the normal social relationships of men. It is believed that in these special communities something nearer spiritual perfection can be attained. Any advantage accruing to the world outside from this withdrawal by some of its members into spiritual 'religious' communities is mainly accidental, their prime purpose being to promote the spiritual well-being of their own members and save other men by bringing them out of the world into the special religious community. The full rigour of this kind of doctrine is to be found, however, not in Roman Catholic Christianity but in Hinduism of the most serious sort.

(3) A third kind of perfectionism is represented by those individuals or groups, usually Protestant, who believe that the immediate practice of the absolute law of love is possible in ordinary society, and accept all the essentials of a normal social and natural life in the family, working for a living and all that goes with them. These take a strongly optimist view of the immediate possibilities open to men to recreate their life on earth in the pattern of God's perfect will. An example of the naïve optimism of this way of thinking comes to

mind from the dark days before the Second World War, about 1932. At that time the Japanese wantonly attacked Shanghai and were heroically opposed by the Chinese. In Britain a Peace Army was formed under religious leadership, and offered itself to go between the contending forces and persuade them to desist and be reconciled. The offer was not accepted and the experiment was left untried. What was wrong with such a plan was its fantastic underestimate of the strength of the greed and carelessness of human life that had led the Japanese to their wholly unprovoked attack on the Chinese, the strength of the habit of obedience in the Japanese soldier, the strength of the conviction in the Chinese who fought that they were upholding their just cause in doing so. One may well believe that, if the Japanese had been influenced by an intervention of this kind to desist from their attack, it would have been from fear of the complications that might ensue with the military power of Britain rather than out of regard for the self-sacrificing love of the members of the Peace Army. A naïve optimistic perfectionism tends to make little or no impression on the real world.

The purpose of this chapter has been to show that Christian ethical realism accepts the law of love as demanding the best, the very best, that can be done, starting from where we are, to express love effectively in the world of actual human relationships. Love, without qualification, is the test of what should be done, but always the application is to actual concrete circumstances—this situation, and not some other. So out of love Jesus received some tenderly, others with hard conditions, scorched the self righteous and the cruel with criticism, overthrew the money-changers, submitted to the power of Pilate, varying his action to the needs of the situation, but never abandoning the test and motive of love.

When we come to consider the real situation in which

Christian love is called upon to find expression in politics, certain features are fairly clear.

It should be plain from what has been said that the attempt to exercise Christian judgment in action in democratic countries today is obligatory on all, but will vary according to the situation of the individual. There is no absolute standpoint above the battle from which the Christian, as an individual, or the Church corporately, can influence the development of the community. It is always evident when any economic or political question is discussed in Presbytery or General Assembly that all the members see the issues from special standpoints. Everyone is limited by special interests and sympathies. The attempt to reach a view that is simply Christian and therefore, ideally, one that can command the assent of all sincere Christians, usually ends in a compromise that is either vague or contradictory, and consequently almost useless as a guide to action. One limitation, which amounts almost to a disqualification of the Church as a body in this field is that the Church as such has no direct responsibility for action. This is very evident in the deliberations of any such body as the Church of Scotland's Assembly Committee on Church and Nation. It has no executive power, nor has it at its disposal the guidance of well-informed experts on the various questions it discusses. It tends, therefore, to range over a very wide field of interests without being able to give to any of its conclusions the precision that action requires.

Attempts have been made in some European countries to form Christian democratic political parties, organised to seek electoral support and to exercise governmental power. It is very evident from this experience that the concrete policies pursued by such parties are not in fact the only policies that could commend themselves to a Christian judgment. Some men of not less Christian outlook find themselves in political opposition to the 'Christian' parties, and within these parties are found men who for reasons of their own, unconnected with Christian conviction, give them active support. The 'Christian' parties develop their own special set of interests and habits of mind. Generally they are marked indeed by moderation and a sense of responsibility. But there are different ways of being moderate and responsible, and in some issues, moderation may itself be un-Christian. Further it is always in danger of degenerating into indecision. In short, there is no way in which a political party in a democracy can be unambiguously and decisively Christian. Even a party calling itself Christian is not likely to be different from any other party in bringing together in one organisation, a mixture of motives and personalities, good and evil.

Furthermore experience suggests that in any society there is need both for conservation and reconstruction or reform, and that any man's appreciation of what is needful will be controlled by diverse factors of temperament, intelligence, experience and circumstance. Each of us is capable of seeing only part of the problem in a complex society; each is capable of making only a limited contribution to its solution. All this would suggest that it is inevitable that a genuine Christian judgment may lead one man to associate himself with conservative policies, another to radical policies of reform. A genuinely Christian outlook will, however, always have certain marks. It will be realistic in its awareness of sin, of self-interest disguising itself as idealism, of the tortuous self-deception of the human mind in himself and others, of the pretensions of the righteous. It will display a special capacity for self-criticism, through submission of all its programmes, policies and tactics to the standards of Christian love. It will know itself to be under the judgment of God and in need of His renewed forgiveness.

Further, Christian judgment will always see its political opponents as *men*, in the fullest sense, men from whom love cannot finally be withheld, and their political life will be purged of all rancour and hatred. Strife will not cease but it will be held within creative limits. If estrangement or hostility develops, it will not be allowed to become fixed and final. Ways of reconciliation will be perseveringly sought.

The Minister and Politics. The relevance of religion to politics and the obligation of a Christian in a democracy to play his part in taking the decisions that his times require places a special and a difficult duty upon ministers of religion.

The minister's special task is to make plain to men and women their fundamental situation of responsibility before God their Creator, Judge and Redeemer, and their relation to their fellow-men in the purpose of God. Nothing should be allowed to interfere with this supreme task. This will ordinarily mean that a minister should never allow himself to be thought of as a politician, even an amateur politician. If he is, then probably for both those who support his politics and those who oppose them, it will be difficult to accept or understand his message as a minister. His supporters will be in great danger of identifying policies with the will of God, the way to self-righteousness and downright wickedness. The opponents will be inclined to reject a gospel obscured for them by association with a policy they abhor.

Yet it should not be concluded that a minister can simply exclude politics from his field of responsibility. It is not permissible, for example, for the minister to pretend that politics and religion are *alternatives* offered to men, and that politics may be dismissed as an absurdly superficial way of dealing with human problems. This is still frequently said in pulpits in relation to the problem of war.[1] It used to be said about the problem of the slums, 'The soul of the slum is the slum in the soul', implying that the way to deal with slums was to *convert* the slum-dweller, or perhaps the slum land-

1. See chapter XI 'The Importance of Institutions'.

lord, and discouraging the direct attack on the problem by slum clearance and state housing programmes. This is now an obsolete position. But in relation to war and, more generally, the hopes attached to political programmes, the foolish rejection of politics is still heard from the pulpit.

The minister must neither be a politician nor simply reject politics. He must so expound and illustrate the meaning of love that those who hear cannot escape the call to express their love in political action according to their best judgment in the situations in which they are placed by the providence of God. There is no reason why a minister should not so preach as to provide inspiration and guidance for political activity to both conservative and reformer in his congregation. There is no reason why there should not be in the same congregation men actively opposed in politics, and each acknowledging the supremacy of the gospel. This is because political questions usually involve judgments of expediency, calculations of consequences and mixed situations, so that there is seldom anything like a pure moral decision involved. Different men acting from similar Christian motives, may have quite different political appreciations of any situation. Nor does this mean that the motive is of no importance.

Again similar policies uniting men in parties may be adopted for different reasons, and so a Christian may find himself co-operating with a non-Christian in opposition politically to a fellow Christian. This, of course, gives rise to problems, because membership of a party always involves submission to its discipline and loyalty to its decisions. Characteristically, the choice is not between good and evil but between a greater and a lesser good (or evil). Recognising this clearly a man may well feel that he can commit himself in all Christian loyalty to the support of a particular party, although he may never be (in the most limited sense) 'a good party man', because his party can never be exempt in his eyes from Christian tests of its policies and actions, and there will always be a tension between his loyalty to his party and his supreme loyalty to God. There are two major moral dangers in the association of politics and religion. On the one hand there is the danger that a political programme may be given the absolute and universal character that belongs only to revelation. Communism, nazism and imperialism all share in this error and sin. On the other hand religion may be betrayed into reliance on political methods and powers. Papalism, ecclesiasticism of any sort, tend towards this form of perversion. There is no way by which men can make themselves finally secure against these dangers. Only God is righteous and we can participate in God's righteousness only by faith, the response to God's righteousness in repentance, obedience and love.

XIV

The Welfare State

DEMOCRACY has moved not perhaps steadily but in the end decisively to the creation of the Welfare State. Two forces have been mainly responsible for this twentieth-century achievement. First, the organised strength of the wage-earning working class has by this means claimed a greater share in the well-being that is open to a modern community. It has secured for itself through the controlling and organising power of the state the services of education, medical skill, security against the worst effects of poverty, sickness, old age, decent housing, and the enjoyment of leisure. The second source of the modern Welfare State is the Christian humanist tradition. It is this that accounts for the compassionate care of the weak: on this side the Welfare State is an extension of the family principle, an application of the Christian teaching that we must 'bear one another's burdens'. It is a recognition that every human being must be counted into the community, and his claim to membership fully acknowledged. As a matter of history it can be said that in Britain these two forces in the modern Welfare State have worked together. The influence of the Christian faith has played a notable part in guiding the rising forces of democracy to measure their claims by moral standards, and not by mere power. At the same time it has influenced the formerly powerful classes to concede the claims of the wage-earning worker not to mere threat but to the pleas of justice and mercy. Thus we have been saved in some degree from the bitterness of civil strife.

Corresponding to these twin sources of the modern Welfare State are two quite different conceptions of its goals, the tests by which its success may be judged.

The first tends to set before the state the task of raising the standard of living. It may tend to repeat the mistake made by men through the ages, the mistake of identifying welfare with wealth. We all fall easily into the mistake of thinking that higher wages, a bigger salary, larger profits, more of the things that money can buy and more leisure to enjoy them will of themselves bring us a better and a happier life. So the Welfare State is usually tested by its success or failure in getting and spending.

A rising standard of living for the average household may be normally a fair enough rough test of the efficiency of government. Yet when we reflect upon it, we know that wealth can be a delusive good. We know, for example, that it is better to marry for love than for money—the true love that lasts, of course, not the intense but superficial and fluctuating passion that the dance tunes call 'Romance'. It is much more important that you should be able to continue to love and trust your wife than that she should be able to give you a generous allowance out of her unearned income.

So the Christian goal and the Christian test for the Welfare State cannot be simply the standard of living it offers. It must be concerned with the human relations enjoyed or promoted in it. If the Welfare State is encouraging a more willing co-operation in worthy common tasks; if it is helping parents to be better parents; if it is eliminating those situations in which some men are the mere tools of others, or being found unprofitable as tools, are neglected or cast aside; if as they grow up children are led into wholesome relations with others, the most important things are being done. 'Seek ye first the Kingdom of God and His righteousness and all these things (material well-being) will be added unto you.' It is only when the foundations of happiness are sound in our relations with one another that wealth is a real addition to happiness. To keep the Welfare State from the delusory progress that has its eyes only on *things*, to sustain the moral purpose that has its eyes on men and women, it must be constantly enlightened by the more profound interpretation of human life that the Christian faith supplies.

It is sometimes suggested that the Welfare State is guilty of a capital mistake in overestimating the capacity of men to do justly and to respond to what we have called the family principle. By taking the burden of the individual on its broad shoulders the Welfare State disguises the hard realities of the economic situation, opens the door to the slacker and welcomes him in to sit cosily by the fire, offers itself for exploitation, fails to apply the discipline that human nature requires and to make use of the natural self-interest that is stimulated by rewards granted to individual effort.

The family principle must not be confused with coddling. No healthy family allows itself to be victimised by a parasitic member. It knows how to make him play his due part in the domestic economy, although in his weakness and failure, even gross moral failure, it rallies to his help.

No more does Christianity deceive itself about men. The Christian doctrine of man recognises the sombre reality of sin It does not think of the state as arising simply out of men's virtues. Rather it sees in the state in one aspect a means appointed by God to limit men's wrongdoing, a means to protect men from one another. It recognises the necessity of the state knowing how to use normal human self-interest in all men to check the inordinate selfishness of some. It knows that the stability and progress of society depend largely on the prudent self-regard and the proper ambition of the good citizen.

The Welfare State of the western world enjoys a standard of living far above that of the great majority of the population of the world. Not only so but to some extent its prosperity has depended upon its ability to exploit the resources of the Asiatic and African continents that contain these vast hungry populations. What has happened within the advanced democratic nations—the advance of the unprivileged to influence and power—is now beginning to happen on a world scale. The formerly subject peoples are claiming independence and the right to advance to equality with the most civilised communities. Already Christian missions, and government, partly guided by moral considerations have gone some distance to anticipate these claims. But often the 'haves' hold out against the claims of the 'have-nots'. That way lies, sooner or later, disastrous strife. Prudence suggests and justice demands that we should in the main concede the claims of the backward peoples. Christian principle suggests that we should assist their advance willingly, in short that that we should go on from the Welfare State to the Welfare World. We should not be afraid to hope and to work as well as to pray for a whole world provided through world government with the means of promoting a co-operative commonwealth embracing all mankind.

There is no finality in human affairs. New problems arise; good institutions become lifeless and corrupt. We cannot by anything we do *secure* the future of mankind. Yet social progress is not an illusion and it is something well worth working for. We have enjoyed its fruits sufficiently to know that we have a duty to bring them within the reach of others.